Ju

D0879792

SOURCES OF CONFIRMATION

FROM THE FATHERS
THROUGH THE REFORMERS

Paul Turner

A Liturgical Press Book

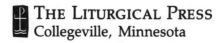

THE LITURGICAL PRESS
Collegeville, Minnesota

Cover design by Ann Blattner.

1   2   3   4   5   6   7   8   9

Library of Congress Cataloging-in-Publication Data

Turner, Paul, 1953–
    Sources of confirmation from the Fathers through the Reformers / Paul Turner.
      p.   cm.
    Includes bibliographical references and index.
    ISBN 0-8146-2006-X
    1. Confirmation—History—Sources. I. Title.
  BV815.T875   1993
  234′.162′09—dc20
                                                        92-32644
                                                          CIP

HUGONI TASCH O.S.B. SODALI
QUI
CONFIRMATIONIS IPSIUS
ANIMIQUE AUCTORIS
ITER
RUDI APERUIT HUIC
HAEC DEDICATUR CATENA

Contents

Abbreviations

ARCEG   *Acta Reformationis Catholicae ecclesiam Germaniae concernentia saeculi xvi: Die Reformverhandlungen des Deutschen Episkopats von 1520 bis 1570.* Ed. Georg Pfeilschifter. Regensburg: Verlag Friedrich Pustet, vol. 1, 1959.

BRHE   *Bibliothéque de la revue d'histoire ecclésiastique.* Louvain: Publications Universitaires de Louvain, vol. 1, 1927.

CCath   *Corpus catholicorum: Werke Katholischer Schriftsteller im Zeitalter der Glaubensspaltung.* Münster in Westfalen: Verlag der Aschendorffschen Verlagsbuchhandlung, vol. 1, 1919.

CChr.CM   *Corpus Christianorum—Continuatio medievalis.* Turnhout: Brepols, vol. 1, 1971.

CChr.SL   *Corpus Christianorum—Series Latina.* Turnhout: Brepols, vol. 1, 1954.

CFI   *Concilium Florentinum documenta et scriptores.* Rome: Pontificium Institutum Orientalium Studiorum, vol. 1, 1940.

CIC   *Corpus Iuris Canonici.* Ed. Emil Friedberg. Editio Lipsiensis secunda. Graz: Akademische Druck-U. Verlagsanstalt, 1955.

COGP   *Concilia omnia, tam generalia, quam particularia, ab apostolorum temporibus in hunc usque diem a sanctissimis patribus celebrata, & quorum acta literis mandata, ex vestustissimis diversarum regionum bibliothecis haberi potuere.* Ed. Petrus Crabbe. Cologne: Petrus Quentel, 1538.

CR   *Corpus reformatorum. Philippi Melanthonis, opera quae supersunt omnia.* Ed. Carolus Gottlieb Bretschneider and Henricus Ernestus Bindseil. 28 vols. Halix Saxonum: C. A. Schwetschke et filium, 1834–1860; reprint ed. New York and London: Johnson Reprint Corporation, 1963.
Ioannis Calvini opera quae supersunt omnia. Ed. Guilielmus Baum et al. Brunsvigae: C. A. Schwetschke et filium, vol. 1 (CR 29) 1863.
Huldreich Zwinglis Sämtliche Werke Unter Mitwirkung des Zwingli-Vereins in Zürich. Ed. Emil Egli, Georg Finsler, Walter Köhler. Leipzig: M. Heinsius Nachfolger, vol. 1 (CR 88) 1905.

CSEL   *Corpus scriptorum ecclesiasticorum Latinorum.* Vienna: F. Tempsky, vol. 1, 1866.

CT   *Concilium Tridentinum Diariorum, Actorum, Epistularum, Tractatuum.* Nova collectio. Ed. Societas Goerresiana. 13 vols. Freiburg: Herder and Co., 1901–1938.

GCS   *Die griechischen christlichen Schriftsteller der ersten drei Jahrhunderte.* Berlin, Leipzig: J. C. Hinrichs'sche Buchhandlung, vol. 1, 1897.

JThS   *Journal of Theological Studies.* Oxford et al.: Clarendon Press, vol. 1, 1899.

Mansi   *Sacrorum conciliorum nova et amplissima collectio.* Ed. Johannes Dominicus Mansi et al. Florence:Antonius Zatta Venetus, vol. 1, 1759.

PG   *Patrologiae cursus completus.* Ed. Jacques-Paul Migne. Series Graeca. Paris: J.-P. Migne, vol. 1, 1857.

PL   *Patrologiae cursus completus.* Ed. Jacques-Paul Migne. Series Latina. Paris: J.-P. Migne. Series Latina. Paris: J.-P. Migne, vol. 1, 1841.

PMAAR   *Papers and Monographs of the American Academy in Rome.* Rome, New Haven: Yale University Press, vol. 1, 1919.

SC   *Sources chrètiennes.* Paris: Editions du Cerf, vol. 1, 1941.

SpicBon *Spicilegium Bonaventurianum.* Quaracchi, Grottaferrata: Editiones Collegii S. Bonaventurae ad Claras Aquas, vol. 1, 1963.

StT   *Studi e Testi.* Vatican City: Biblioteca apostolica Vaticana, vol. 1, 1900.

WA   *D. Martin Luthers Werke. Kritische Gesammtausgabe.* Weimar: Hermann Böhlau, vol. 1, 1883.

WABr   *D. Martin Luthers Werke. Kritische Gesamtausgabe. Briefwechsel.* Weimar: Hermann Böhlaus Nachfolger, vol. 1, 1930.

Preface

The purpose of this book is to offer its readers a collection of texts from which they may follow the course of confirmation from its patristic origins through the Reformation.

The texts collected here represent a variety of sources, including canons from Church councils, theological treatises, rituals, letters, and sermons. These passages describe the origins of confirmation in its ritual celebration and interpretation.

Some references are quite brief and form a tangential portion of a larger argument. I have abbreviated many longer texts to lend balance to the collection. For a complete understanding of each author's intent, I advise the reader to consult the full context.

In some cases such consultation is difficult because the publications are so rare. Indeed, I hope that one contribution of this book will be to place in the reader's hands references not readily accessible in published books or in vernacular languages.

Most of those texts come from the Middle Ages and the Reformation. The material from preceding centuries will frame the background of these later writers.

The reader will note that not all the sources agree about the purpose and celebration of confirmation. This is a feature that frustrates pastoral decisions about the celebration of confirmation in the Roman Catholic Church today. But at the same time it will offer a better understanding about why so many different interpretations of confirmation prevail in the post-Vatican II Church.

This book does not pretend to be a complete collection of sources. Rather, it hopes to be a helpful one by offering certain chains of texts throughout the centuries.

The material is divided in four parts. First appear texts which describe the ritual of confirmation and the candidates for its reception. (The earliest texts, of course, speak of the post-baptismal anointing and/or imposition of hands, before the term "confirmation" came into use.) This chapter puts forth just what the Church did in history.

The second part examines why the Church did it that way. Here appear writings explaining what effects confirmation accomplishes. As a related matter, the concept of irrepeatability occurs in this section. That confirmation cannot be repeated is itself a theological reflection on the rituals of Part I.

Some practical matters about how confirmation is celebrated follow in the third part. Here I have selected three themes: the minister, the matter and form (admittedly a late concept in history), and the mystique of chrism. These themes reflect certain elements of the ritual which grew in importance to the Church over the centuries.

A brief section on the reconciliation of heretics closes the book. Here it is observed that certain elements of the initiation rites were applied to a particular pastoral need in the early Church; namely, how to return to the orthodox fold those who had professed or been baptized in heresies. One might argue that this section illuminates confirmation by showing what it is not. But in the modern Roman Catholic Church, confirmation is still celebrated for those baptized in other Christian Churches who now enter communion with the Roman Church.

Some texts relate to more than one theme and might arguably be placed in a different section from where they will be found. I beg the reader's indulgence if there is disagreement with my choice. The schema is meant to enlighten, not to restrict.

May these and all reflections of history deepen the spirit of the modern Church.

1

RITUALS AND CANDIDATES

Documentation for the origins of confirmation comes from several types of sources. Especially in the early Church, actual ritual texts are scarce. However, references to the rituals are also found in treatises and stories dealing with other subjects. A sample is included below.

By the Middle Ages ritual texts became more widespread and uniform. Prayers are recognized by the few words which begin them. Confirmation has shifted from Easter initiation to a ceremony performed by bishops when they visit churches in their dioceses.

With the coming of the Reformation, confirmation develops a new purpose. Finding inadequate scriptural references, the Reformers discarded the medieval position that confirmation is a sacrament, and carved a place for it as a rite of passage for adolescents. Suggestions come initially from John Calvin and Desiderius Erasmus, then local Churches. True to the Counter-Reform, the Catholic Church retained its opinion regarding the value of confirmation within the sacramental structure.

1. Tertullian (155–220), *On Baptism* 7–8 (c. 198–200)

Then having gone up from the bath we are anointed with a blessed anointing of ancient discipline, by which people were accustomed to be anointed for priesthood, by oil from a horn from which Aaron was anointed by Moses. For this reason we were called "christs" ("anointed ones") from "chrism," which is the ointment which lends its name to the Lord.

11

It was made spiritual because the Lord was anointed with the Spirit by God the Father, as it says in Acts: "For they were gathered together in that city against your holy Son whom you have anointed." Thus also the anointing flows on us physically, but benefits spiritually, as the physical act of baptism (that we are immersed in water) has a spiritual effect (that we are freed from transgressions).

Next, calling and inviting the Holy Spirit, the hand is imposed for the blessing.

CSEL 1:282f.

2. Tertullian, *On the Prescription of Heretics* 36, 4–5 (200?)

Let us see what the Church has learned, and what she has taught: After she also befriended the Churches among the Africans, she knows the one God, the Lord, the Creator of the universe, and Jesus Christ, born of the virgin Mary, son of God the Creator, and the resurrection of the flesh. She blends the law and the prophets with evangelical and apostolic writings, from which she drinks faith. She signs faith with water, dresses it with the Holy Spirit, feeds it with the Eucharist, exhorts it toward martyrdom, and thus accepts no one contrary to this arrangement.

CSEL 1:217.

3. Tertullian, *Against Marcion*, 14,3 (207–212?)

But up to now Jesus has not rejected the water of the Creator, by which he washes his own, nor the oil, by which he anoints his own, nor the mixture of honey and milk, by which he nurses his own, nor bread, in which he presents his very own body.

CSEL 1:455.

4. Hippolytus (+235), *Apostolic Tradition* 21–22 (c. 215)

The neophytes are anointed by the presbyter from the oil consecrated by the bishop. He says, "I anoint you with holy oil in the name of Jesus Christ." And thus, drying themselves, the individuals are vested, and afterwards are brought in the church.

But the bishop, imposing his hand on them, prays by saying, "Lord God, who made them worthy to merit the forgiveness of sins by the bath of rebirth of the Holy Spirit, send your grace onto them, that they may serve you according to your will. For to you is the glory, to the Father and to the Son with the Holy Spirit in the holy Church, both now and for ever. Amen."

Afterwards, pouring the consecrated oil from his hand and imposing it on the neophyte's head, let him say, "I anoint you with holy oil in the Lord, the Father Almighty, and Christ Jesus, and the Holy Spirit."

And consigning the neophyte on the forehead, let him offer the kiss and say, "The Lord be with you." And let those who have been signed say, "And also with you." Let him do the same to each individual.

SC 11bis:86–90.

5. Eusebius (c. 263–340), *History of the Church* 3, 23; 6, 43 (312–325?)

(Eusebius cites *The Rich Man Who Finds Salvation* by Clement, for a story about John the apostle, who entrusted a young man to the care of the bishop of Smyrna.)

John then returned to Ephesus, and the cleric took home the youngster entrusted to his care, brought him up, kept him in his company, looked after him, and finally gave him the grace of baptism. After this he relaxed his constant care and watchfulness, having put upon him the seal of the Lord as the perfect protection.

(Eusebius quotes a letter from Cornelius to Fabius, explaining the conditions under which Novatus was baptized.)

The occasion of his becoming a believer came from Satan, who entered into him and stayed within him a considerable time. While the exorcists were trying to help him he fell desperately ill, and since he was thought to be on the point of death, there as he lay in bed he received baptism by affusion—if it can be called baptism in the case of such a man.

And when he recovered he did not receive the other things of which one should partake according to the rule of the Church, in particular the sealing by a bishop. Without receiving these how could he receive the Holy Ghost?

The History of the Church from Christ to Constantine, trans. G. A. Williamson, Bungay (Penguin Books, 1965) 129, 282f.

6. Basil (c. 330–379), *On the Holy Spirit* 15, 35 (c. 375)

(Basil argues that some practices come to us from traditions, not from specific writings. He illustrates with the details of the baptismal ritual.)

We also bless the water of baptism, the oil of anointing, and even the baptized themselves. By virtue of what writings? Is it not by virtue of the protected, secret, and hidden tradition? Indeed! Even the oil of anointing, what written word has taught about that? The triple immersion, from where does it come? And everything that surrounds baptism: the renunciation of Satan and his angels—from what Scripture does that come?

Is it not from that teaching held private and secret, which our fathers kept in silence, protected from anxiety and curiosity, knowing well that in keeping quiet one safeguards the sacred character of the mysteries? For how would it be reasonable to divulge by writing the instruction, that which is not permitted to the unitiatiated to contemplate?

SC 17bis:234f.

7. Ambrose (334?–397), *On the Mysteries* 6, 29; 7, 42 (390?)

After these things you went up to the priest. Consider what followed. Was it not that which David said? "As ointment on the head which flows down onto the beard, the beard of Aaron (Ps 133:2)." This is the ointment of which Solomon also said, "Your name is an ointment poured out; therefore young women have loved you and drawn toward you (Song 1:2)." Today, how many renewed souls have loved you, Lord Jesus, saying, "Draw us to you. We hasten to the aroma of your garments (Song 1:3)," that they may breathe the aroma of resurrection.

Therefore recall that you received a spiritual sign, "the spirit of wisdom and understanding, the spirit of counsel and strength, the spirit of knowledge and piety, the spirit of holy fear (Is 11:2-3)," and preserve what you have received. God the Father signed you, Christ the Lord confirmed you and gave the spirit as a pledge in your hearts, as you have learned in the apostolic reading (2 Cor 1:21-22).

SC 25:117, 121.

8. Prudentius (348–405?), *Hymn before Sleep* 125–128 (401–403?)

Worshipper of God, remember that you underwent the holy dew of the font and the bath; you were marked by chrism.

CChr.SL 126:33.

9. Augustine (354–430), *On the First Epistle of John, to Parthos* 6, 10 (413–418?)

In the early days the Holy Spirit fell upon believers. They spoke in tongues which they had not learned, as the Spirit gave them to pronounce. The signs were appropriate for the time. For it was necessary that the Holy Spirit be so signified in all languages, because the gospel of God had run through all languages in the whole world. This was signified, and it took place.

Now is this expected, that those people speak in tongues on whom the hand is imposed that they may receive the Holy Spirit? Or when we impose the hand on these neophytes, does each of you expect that they will speak in tongues? And when you saw that they did not speak in tongues, was any of you so perverse in the heart that you said, "These did not receive the Holy Spirit; for if they had received it, they would be speaking in tongues as happened back then"? If then through these miracles alone there be no testimony of the presence of the Holy Spirit, how does it happen that people know they have received the Holy Spirit?

Ask your heart: If it loves its brothers and sisters, the Spirit of God remains in it.

SC 75:298.

10. Augustine, *Sermon* 227, 1

Baptism and water have come. You have been penetrated, as it were, so that you may come to the form of bread. But it is not yet bread without fire. What therefore does fire represent? It is chrism. For the oil of our fire is the sacrament of the Holy Spirit.

PL 38:1100.

11. Augustine, *On the Trinity* 15:26,46 (420?)

Nor did any of Jesus' disciples give the Holy Spirit. Indeed, they prayed that it might come to those on whom they imposed the hand, but they themselves were not giving it. The Church now preserves this custom in her overseers. . . . And in the Acts of the Apostles it is written more evidently about this matter: "Because God anointed him with the Holy Spirit," not with visible oil, but with the gift of grace which is signified by the visible ointment by which the Church anoints the baptized.

CChr.SL 50A:526.

12. Pseudo-Dionysius (431–451?), *The Ecclesiastical Hierarchy* 2:2, 7; 2:3, 8; 7:3, 11

At this point, the bishop orders the ones to be baptized to give a threefold profession, he receives the profession with a third blessing, and imposes the hand on them. And while the ministers lead them out from within, the priests bring forth the sacred oil of anointing.

But the bishop, beginning the anointing with a triple sign, hands those to be baptized to the priests, to be completely anointed on the whole body. He himself goes to the mother of adoption, that is the font. After he has sanctified its waters with sacred invocations, consecrated it with three pourings of the most sacred ointment in the form of the cross, and with as many applications of the sacred oil, singing a most sacred hymn of divine inspiration to the God of inspiring prophets, he orders those to be baptized to be brought forth.

And while a priest someplace announces from what is written both them and the sponsors, the initiates are led by the hands of priests into the water to the hand of the bishop. Standing above where the priests behind the waters proclaim toward the bishop the names of those to be baptized, the bishop immerses them three times by invoking the three Persons of divine beatitude under this threefold immersion and emersion.

Then drawing them out, the other priests hand them over to the sponsors, or the minister of admission, and when together with them they have wrapped the newly baptized with fitting garments, they lead them back to the bishop.

He, signing them with divinely consecrated oil, declares them participants of the most sacred Eucharist.

Then they clothe the initiated with white vestments. . . . Then that perfecting oil of anointing bathes the newly baptized with the sweetness of its aroma. For the sacred initiation of divine generation joins the things which have been begun to the divine Spirit.

I believe that there is nothing absurd if children are led to the divine instruction, if they have a leader and sponsor who endows them with knowledge of divine matters, and keeps them safe from adversities. Furthermore, a bishop makes children sharers of the sacred mysteries that they may be taught in them, lest they lead another life which only observes that which is divine. And let them come to holy communion. In these ways they may possess a sacred habit, and may be promoted diligently by the sponsor.

PG 3:395f; 403f; 567f.

13. Gregory of Tours (538-594), *On the Glory of the Martyrs* 41

(Gregory proclaims the power of faith and the Christian name in a scene of martyrdom in which the Emperor Diocletian describes the appearance of a Christian.)

Then the emperor himself, after his crown has been removed, says, "Who is this opposed to our gods, and friend of the Christian religion, who bears a forehead signed with the inscription of chrism, and adores the wood of the cross? Do not delay to make it known."

PL 71:742.

14. Pope Eugene I (654–657)

In the catechumenate, in baptism, and in confirmation the same godparent may be used if necessity demands. Nonetheless it is not a Roman custom, where each ritual has its own.

CIC 1:1394. (Gratian: c. 100, D.4, de cons.)

15. Council of Constantinople III, canon 7 (680)

Candidates cannot become catholics unless they memorize the creed and the Lord's prayer, believe them with all their heart, and frequent them most often in prayer. For it has been established by the holy fathers that unless people memorize these, they may not be chrismated, nor baptized, nor may they sponsor another at the bath of the font, nor hold whomever they please before the bishop for confirmation. Excused are those whose age has led them to speaking little.

Mansi 11:1008f.

16. Alcuin (735–804), *On the Divine Offices* 19

Then the priest baptizes the neophytes under a triple immersion, by invoking the Holy Trinity only once, saying, "And I baptize you in the name of the Father," and he immerses once; "and of the Son," and he immerses again; "and of the Holy Spirit," and he immerses a third time.

Then as he comes up from the font, the presbyter makes the sign of the cross in chrism with his thumb on the crown of the neophyte's head, saying this prayer: "Almighty God, Father of our Lord Jesus Christ." Then the neophytes are taken up by the ones by whom they must be taken up; afterwards they are dressed in their clothes.

But if the bishop is there it is necessary that they be confirmed with chrism at once, and afterwards that they receive communion. If the bishop is absent, they may receive communion from the presbyter saying, "May the Body of our Lord Jesus Christ preserve you into eternal life. Amen." Some godparents are accustomed to draw their children from the font, but that is not found in the rituals.

Concerning this matter the apostolic Church acted in this way among the Romans. After the bishop baptized, or whoever he ordered to do it, they lifted the neophytes themselves in their hands and offered them to one of the priests. But he himself then makes the cross in chrism on the crown of their head with his thumb, saying, "Almighty God, Father of our Lord Jesus Christ," as above.

When these things are completed, those who will take them up have been prepared with linen cloths in their hands. Then they receive them from the bishop or the deacons who had baptized them. Then after they have been dressed, they are brought to the bishop for confirming. He gives them each the white stole, the chrisom, and ten small coins, and thus they are dressed.

And after they have been clad the bishop gives the prayer over them, namely with a hand imposed over their heads, with the invocation of the sevenfold grace of the Holy Spirit. The prayer is "Almighty eternal God, who deigned to give new birth" (*cf. #20 below*). When this prayer is over, he makes the cross in chrism with his thumb on each forehead, saying, "In the name of the Father, and of the Son, and of the Holy Spirit. Peace be with you." All should respond, "And also with you." These are the words of salvation for the new person, who is reborn. . . .

PL 101:1219f.

17. Decretum Compendiense (757), Council of Verberie

If any man presents his stepson or stepdaughter to the bishop for confirmation, he may be separated from his wife and never receive another. Similarly also a woman.

CIC 1:1096. (Gratian, c. 2, C.30, q. 1)

18. Pope Nicholas (858–867), *Letter to Rudolph* (864)

Concerning those who present their stepchildren for confirmation before bishops, that is, those who hold up on themselves the children of their wife from her first husband, while they are chrismated by bishops—if with ignorance as you maintain, let it be, although it is a sin. Nevertheless it must not be punished up to the separation of the spouse. However, let them weep, and washing this away with worthy penance for the Lord, let them say, "Do not remember the sins of our ignorance."

CIC 1:1098. (Gratian, c. 6, C. 30, q. 1)

19. Pseudo-Council of Orleans (9th c.?), canon 3

Those fasting should come to confirmation at a mature age. They should be admonished to make a confession first, that being upright they may be worthy to receive the gift of the Holy Spirit, because one will never be a Christian unless he or she will have been chrismated with episcopal confirmation.

CIC 1:1414. (Gratian, c. 68, D. 5, de cons.)

20. The Roman Ritual (10th c.), *Holy Saturday* 99, 385–387

Then while the archdeacon holds the chrism, the bishop comes to the neophytes. Their shoulders and arms are covered with a linen cloth. The bishop, having lifted up and imposed his hand on the heads of all, gives the prayer over them with the invocation for the sevenfold grace of the Holy Spirit.

Prayer. "Almighty eternal God, who deigned to give rebirth to these your servants out of water and the Holy Spirit, who gave them forgiveness of all their sins, send onto them the sevenfold Holy Spirit, your Paraclete, from the heavens, the Spirit of wisdom and understanding, the Spirit of counsel and fortitude, the Spirit of knowledge and piety, fill them with the Spirit of fear of you and consign them with the sign of the cross of Christ in gracious eternal life." All respond, "Amen."

When the prayer has been finished, the deacons ask the names of each. The bishop, his thumb having been dipped in chrism, makes the cross on the foreheads of each, saying, "I confirm and consign you in the name of the Father and of the Son, and of the Holy Spirit." All respond, "Amen." "Peace be with you." All respond, "And also with you." Then he says these verses to all who have been confirmed, "Behold thus is the one blessed who fears the Lord. . . ."

StT 227:109.

21. Hugh of St. Victor (+1142), *On the Sacraments* 2:7,6

How much time those who receive the imposition of the hand ought to be under the instruction of chrism.

Some frequently ask how much time they ought to keep the anointing of chrism on the head; namely, that those who receive the imposition of the hand not wash their heads, after the time at the baptistry.

To them it may be responded that it is fitting that as much time as the coming of the Holy Spirit upon the apostles is generally celebrated by the Church, so much time may the coming of the Holy Spirit be celebrated by anyone who receives him; that is, for seven days. And deservedly, because seven are the gifts of the Holy Spirit, and the Holy Spirit comes to his guest in seven assemblies. And it is right that each gift has its own day and that a banquet be prepared for each on its day. Wisdom has one day, understanding another, counsel another, fortitude another, knowledge another, piety another, and fear another. Christ makes use of such banquets with his guests; so does the Holy Spirit.

PL176:462.

22. William Duranti (c. 1230–1296), *On Confirmation*

After the candidate has indeed been chrismated on the forehead, his head is bound with a white linen band, lest the running oil flow down or off. It ought to be worn for seven days, because of the seven gifts of the Holy Spirit, who is received in this sacrament.

But because it would be dangerous to wear chrism on the forehead for so long a time, we permit in substitution that priests may remove the bands on the third day, burn them up upon the fonts, and wash the foreheads, or they may fashion a taper of these bands and they may be offered on the altar. But the head of another to be confirmed may be bound with the same band.

> *Instructions et constitutions de Guillaume Durand le spéculateur d'après le manuscrit de Cessenon.* Ed. Jos. Berthelé, M. Valmary. Archives du Départment de l'Hérault: Documents et Inventaires complémentaires. Montpellier: Imprimerie Delord-Boehm et Martial, 1900, 16.

23. William Duranti, *The Roman Pontifical of the Middle Ages*, and *Ritual 50*, Concerning Children to be Chrismated on the Forehead

The bishop intending to chrismate children on the forehead, prepared with alb, stole, white chasuble, and mitre, sends out a reminder as it may be called in the Notice concerning parishes needing to be visited. Then, after the thumb of his right hand has been washed and dried, while those to be confirmed are kneeling down with their hands joined before their heart, the bishop, standing, his mitre removed, similarly with hands joined before his heart, says, "May the Holy Spirit come upon you and the power of the Most High keep you from sins." All respond, "Amen."

Then he says, "Our help is in the name of the Lord. Lord, hear my prayer. The Lord be with you. And also with you. Let us pray." And then, after his hands have been raised and extended over those to be confirmed, he says, "Almighty, eternal God, who deigned to give rebirth to these your servants . . . in gracious eternal life (*cf. #20 above*). Through Christ our Lord." All respond, "Amen."

Then, as the bishop sits on the faldstool before the altar or prepared in another place, those needing to be consigned are presented to him by the sponsor after the name of each one has been requested one by one. After the tip of the thumb of his right hand has been dipped in chrism, the bishop makes the cross on each one's forehead, saying, "John," or "Mary," or with whatever other name, "I sign you with the sign of the cross and I confirm you with the chrism of salvation. In the name of the Father and of the Son, and of the Holy Spirit, that you may be filled with the same Holy Spirit and have eternal life." Each responds, "Amen." And while saying, "In the name of the Father and of the Son and of the Holy Spirit," he draws the sign of the cross on each one's face.

And then he lightly delivers a slap on the cheek, saying, "Peace be with you."

When all have been thus consigned, he dries his thumb with a bit of bread or a linen cloth and washes it with water over some tin cup or basin. The water of washing with the linen cloth or bread is thrown in the fonts or the pool. And again the antiphon is sung, "Confirm, O God, what you have worked in us from your holy temple which is in Jerusalem." The versicle is, "Glory to the Father. As it was in the beginning." And then the antiphon "Confirm" is repeated.

Then the bishop arising, standing with his mitre removed, says the versicle "Show us. Lord hear. The Lord be with you." The prayer which he says with hands joined before his heart and while all the confirmed kneel devoutly is, "God, who gave your apostles the Holy Spirit. . . ." All respond, "Amen."

Then he says, "Behold thus is blessed the one who fears the Lord." And making the sign of the cross over them, he says, "May the Lord bless you from Sion and may you see good things in Jerusalem all the days of your life, and may you have eternal life." All respond, "Amen."

After confirmation has thus unfolded, the bishop announces to the confirmed or chrismated that in honor of the Holy Trinity, they should wear the chrism band on their foreheads for three days, and on the third day the priest will wash their foreheads and burn the bands upon the fonts, or they may make a taper from them for the use of the altar. Then he announces to the sponsors that they should instruct and form their godchildren in good morals and deeds, that they may flee from evil things and do good. They should also teach them the Creed, the Our Father, and the Hail Mary, since they oblige themselves to this, as is contained more fully in our "Synodal Constitutions."

StT 88:333–335.

24. Philipp Melanchthon (1497–1560), Theological Topics (1521)

There was once an examination of doctrine in which individuals used to recite a summary of doctrine and showed that they dissented from Gentiles and heretics. It was a very useful way of educating people, likewise for separating the profane and the religious. Afterwards it became a public prayer, and the apostles imposed hands on them. Thus they were being presented with manifest gifts of the Holy Spirit.

But now the rite of confirmation, which bishops retain, is an utterly empty ceremony. It would be useful however that an investigation and profession of doctrine be made and a public prayer for the sake of religious people, nor would that prayer be futile.

CR 21:853.

25. Desiderius Erasmus of Rotterdam (1465–1536), *Paraphrases on the New Testament, "To the Devoted Reader"* (1522)

It seems to me that this rite would not be conducted indifferently, if baptized children, when they will have arrived at puberty, are asked to be present for gatherings of this kind, in which is explained to them clearly what the profession of baptism contains in itself. Then they are examined diligently in private by upright men, whether they sufficiently hold and have memorized those things which the priest taught.

If they learn to remember enough, they are asked whether they have fulfilled what their sponsors promised in their name at baptism. If they respond that they have fulfilled it, then that profession is publicly renewed, as equals gathered, in ceremonies which are solemn, appropriate, pious, serious, and grand. These things befit that profession, than which nothing can be holier. . . .

These rituals will have more authority if they are done by bishops themselves, not by pastors or assembled suffragans.

Desiderii Erasmi Roterodami Opera Omnia (Lyons: Petrus Vander Aa, 1706), vol. 7. Third unnumbered page of introduction.

26. Martin Luther (1483–1546), *Sermon on the Afternoon of Laetare Sunday* (15 March 1523)

Confirmation as the bishops want it should not be bothered with. Nevertheless we do not fault any pastor who might scrutinize the faith from children. If it be good and sincere, he may impose hands and confirm.

WA 11:66.

27. John Calvin (1509–1564), *Principles of the Christian Religion* 4:19,4 (1536)

This was once the custom, that the children of Christians after they had grown up were stood up before the bishop that they might fulfill that duty which was required of those adults who were offering them for baptism. . . .

Therefore, those who had been initiated at baptism as infants, because they had not then performed a confession of faith before the Church towards the end of childhood—or as adolescence was beginning—were again presented by the parents, were examined by the bishop according to a formula of catechism which people held definite and universal.

But so that this action, which otherwise deservedly ought to have been weighty and holy, might have all the more of reverence and dignity, the ceremony of the imposition of hands was also being used.

CR 30:1068.

28. Martin Luther, *Letter to Pastor Gregor Solinus in Tangermünde, Wittenberg, 13 September 1540,* No. 3534

If you wish you will also be able to anoint the sick and confirm adults at times, because the prince denies that they are sacraments, and he established the simple ceremony with a clear conscience.

WABr 9:232.

29. Colloquy of Ratisbon, *On Confirmation* (1540)

And because now all infants are baptized and do not bring forth by themselves the profession of faith at baptism, it is fitting that children, after having been catechized and instructed concerning the religion of Christ, are brought forward to receive the sacrament of confirmation, and confess faith in Christ and obedience to the Church by their own mouth, in the way established by the Council of Orleans, canon 3 (which is found in Gratian, De consecratione dist. V cap 6., "Ut ieiuni" [*cf. #19 above*]), so that the custom observed up to now in other Churches may not be condemned until it is established by the general council over it.

ARCEG 6:68.

30. John Eck (1486–1543), *On the Sacrament of Confirmation* (1542)

I reject that whole appendage (of Bucer), unless the author turns himself back in the end, because children baptized and confirmed have greater grace than those baptized only. It follows that children baptized and confirmed when dying are designated to be rewarded with the greater glory of blessing, of which one degree excels all the riches of the world. Therefore confirmation should be hastened for infants, says Holcot and Maioris.

Nor should it be necessary to expect the use of reason, says Gerson. He cites the Council of Orleans, canon 3 (*cf. #19 above*). Gratian cited it as well, also Ivo in Panormia. Nevertheless in the printed Council of Orleans it is not found. If it is found it says the canon speaks about adults who are of a mature age and ought to come fasting to confirmation, after the confession of sins has first been made.

Apologia pro reverendis. et illustris. principibus Catholicis. ac alijs ordinibus Imperij aduersus mucores & calumnias Buceri, super actis Comitiorum Ratisponae. Ingolstadt: 1542. Fol. xxxxv.

31. Friedrich Nausea (1490–1552), *On Confirmation*, Book 3, *"On the Ritual and Means of the Ceremonies Customarily Used in Confirming People,"* chapter 29

Then the bishop strikes the one thus confirmed on the cheek, not for some disdaining motives. . . . This slap represents the imposition of hands that the apostles used in confirming. Nothing else is now conferred by a bishop than was once conferred by the apostles.

Catholicus catechismus. Cologne: Quentelianus, 1543. Fol. xxx.

32. Martin Bucer (1491–1551), *On the Reign of Christ* I, 7

Instead we read that the early Churches used the sign of imposing the hand, both in the reconciliation of penitents and in the confirmation of the baptized in the faith of Christ, which bishops used to do according to the example of the apostles who were conferring the Holy Spirit on the baptized with this sign (Acts 8). Therefore, those who desire that the kingdom of Christ be justly restored before themselves ought to take care first of all that the rightful administration of baptism and Eucharist be recalled.

Ed. François Wendel, Opera Latina 15 (Paris: Presses Universitaires de France, 1955) Liber I, caput VII, "De sacramentorum dispensatione," 66.

33. Martin Bucer, *Opinions on the Book of Common Prayer*

Finally, it is ordered in this place that no one be admitted to holy communion unless he or she has been confirmed. This precept will be exceedingly salutary if also people be not solemnly confirmed unless they have confirmed the confession of their mouth with a proper life, and if it can be known also from their morals that they are making a confession of their own faith and not another's.

E. C. Whitaker, *Martin Bucer and the Book of Common Prayer: Censura Martini Buceri Super Libro Sacrorum Seu Ordinationis Ecclesiae atque Ministerii Ecclesiastici in Regno Angliae ad petitionem R. Archiepiscopi Cantuarensis Thomae Cranmeri Conscripta,* Alcuin Club Collection, No. 55 (Great Wakering: Mayhew-McCrimmon, 1974) 115.

34. Wittenberg Reformation of 1545

This would be highly necessary in all Churches—to keep the *Catechism* on the appointed day, to instruct the youth in all the necessary articles of Christian teaching. Here confirmation might be prepared; namely, as a child comes to its mature years, to hear openly its confession of faith, and to ask whether it wishes to live by only these godly and ecclesial teachings, and after the confession and questioning to say a prayer with the imposition of hands. This would be a useful ceremony, not only in appearance, but much more in upholding right learning and clear understanding and in good wholesome upbringing.

CR 5:584.

35. The Leipzig Interim (1548), *Confirmation*

Confirmation is taught and retained. Especially the mature youth are asked their faith by their bishops or whomever these direct, that they may confess it to them, and confirm the promise which their sponsors made for them at baptism, having renounced the devil. Thus they are confirmed and sustained in their faith by means of godly grace, with the imposition of hands and Christian prayers and ceremonies.

CR 7:261.217.

36. Order of Confirmation, St. Nicholas of Strassbourg Church (c. 1550)

Such a Christian and altogether necessary ceremony is once more provided in the Church, whereby baptized children after they have now learned the catechism are openly brought before the Church and after an open and voluntary confession submit to the discipline and obedience of the Church with hand-laying and faithful prayer to commend them to the Lord our God and his dear congregation.

Quoted from J. D. C. Fisher, *Christian Initiation: The Reformation Period. Some Early Reformed Rites of Baptism and Confirmation and Other Contemporary Documents,* Alcuin Club Collections, No. 51 (London: S.P.C.K., 1970) 175.

37. Johannes Brenz (1499–1570), *On the Sacraments: On Baptism (1561)*

Then we teach that those who are baptized in the name of the Father and of the Son and of the Holy Spirit are anointed with spiritual chrism; that is, they become members of Christ through faith and are endowed with the Holy Spirit, that the ears of their minds may be opened for hearing heavenly things, and the eyes of their hearts may be illumined. . . .

And the use of external chrism pertains to the elements of the world. . . . And Dionysius, whom they call the Areopagite, and whom they think had transcribed the rites of the Church handed down from the apostles, indicates that external chrism was indeed used in the Church, but indicates also that not at all obscurely this rite was taken up partly from the athletic anointings of the Gentiles and partly from the Mosaic law. . . .

Furthermore, how can the making or the rite of external chrism be handed down by apostles themselves or truly confirmed as Fabian writes (*cf. #170 below*), since the Acts of the Councils witness that this rite was instituted by Sylvester (*cf. #153 below*)?

"Confessio illustrissimi Principis ac Domini, D. Christophori Ducis Wirtembergensis, & Theccensis, Comitis Montebeligardi, &c (1561)." *Corpus et Syntagma Confessionum Fidei quae in diversis regnis et nationibus, ecclesiarum nomine fuerunt authenticé editae: in celeberrimis Conuentibus exhibitae, publicáque auctoritate comprobatae.* Editio Nova. Geneva: Petri Chovet, 1654. 2:109.

38. Martin Chemnitz (1522–1586), *Examination of the Council of Trent, On Confirmation*, 25 (1566)

The rite of confirmation may be used in this way; namely, that those who were baptized in infancy (for such is now the situation for the Church), when they have arrived at the years of discretion, be instructed diligently in the certain and simple catechesis of the doctrine of the Church. And if they seem to have received the beginnings indifferently, they are later offered to the bishop and the Church.

There the children baptized in infancy are first impressed with the brief and simple reminder of their baptism—namely, where they were baptized, how, why, and into what they were baptized, that in that baptism the whole Trinity joined and signed them. That was the covenant of peace and the pact of grace. They are reminded how the renunciation of Satan took place there, the profession of faith, and the promise of obedience.

Second, the children themselves bring forth before their own Church the public profession of this doctrine and of the faith.

Third, they are questioned about particular topics of the Christian religion, and they respond to individual points. But if they understand something poorly they are instructed rightly.

Fourth they are reminded, and they show by this profession, that they separate themselves from all pagan, heretic, fanatic, and profane opinions.

Fifth, a grave and serious exhortation from the word of God is added, that they may persevere in the pact of baptism and in that doctrine and faith, and they may be confirmed by continually advancing.

Sixth, a public prayer is made for these children, that God may deign to govern, preserve, and confirm them in this profession by his Holy Spirit. The imposition of hands may be bestowed at this prayer without superstition. Nor is this a futile prayer, for it shines with promises about the gift of perseverance and the grace of confirmation.

Examen Concilii Tridentini. Ed. Preuss. Berlin: Gust. Schlawitz, 1861, 297.

39. Surius (1522–1578) 1, Life of Rembert

But it is also told, in the custom of the early saints, that Rembert (888) performed certain miracles. Namely, when he traveled to Sweden, he frequently calmed the storm of the sea by his prayers, he gave sight to the eyes of a certain blind man, and that he confirmed him with the pontifical custom when the sacred chrism had been applied.

Historiae seu vitae sanctorum. Turin: Eq. Petri Marietti, 1875. 2:104.

40. Robert Bellarmine (1542–1621), On the Sacrament of Confirmation 2 (1588)

In order that I may omit what must be said below concerning chrism, it is false that the imposition of the hand has been also rejected. For the bishop twice imposes hands on those to be confirmed, as may be understood from the Roman pontifical: once when he extends his hands over them and prays; and again when he signs and anoints the forehead. Since that anointing and signation is done with the hand, it is most rightly called the imposition of the hand, as Hugh teaches in book 2 concerning the sacraments, part 7, chapter 2 (*cf. #21 above*).

Disputationum de Controversiis Christianae fidei adversus hujus temporis haereticos. 6 vols. Naples: Josephum Giuliano and Milan: Natale Battezzati, 1857–1862. Vol. 3 (1858) 216.

2

THEOLOGICAL REFLECTIONS

A. THE EFFECTS

Theologians and catechists of the early Church wanted the newly baptized to understand the mystery into which they were initiated. Their treatises, essays, and homilies explained the parts of the initiation rites in more detail.

Most reflections concern two related fonts, the Scriptures and the ritual itself. They provide a rich means for unfolding the experience of the baptized and the faith of the Church.

The ritual initiation carries moral implications for the faithful. The newly baptized are encouraged to moral fidelity in the life they have chosen.

Since the ritual gestures borrow imagery of the Holy Spirit, the texts which follow reflect deeply on the role of the Spirit in the Trinity, the Church, and the Christian.

By the Middle Ages confirmation has come to be celebrated apart from baptism when children have reached a more mature age. This pastoral reality engendered a whole theology of confirmation as a military sacrament that arms one for the struggle of life.

In the Churches of the Reform, delaying confirmation to some years after baptism gave the leaders a chance to ascertain if children had appropriated for themselves the faith spoken for them in baptism at their infancy.

41. Clement of Alexandria (c. 150–215), *Paidagogos* 1:6, 26, 1–2

(Clement speaks about the perfection achieved in baptism. He explores the image of anointing, though without reference to the ritual itself.)

When we are baptized, being relieved of the faults which, like a cloud, make an obstacle to the Holy Spirit, we restore freely, without a veil and luminous, that eye of the spirit which alone lets us contemplate the divine. For the Holy Spirit coming from heaven is poured on us. It is an anointing of eternal clarity capable of making us see eternal light, for one is a friend to whatever is similar.

SC 70:158.

42. Justin (+165), *Questions and Answers to the Orthodox*, 137

Question: If before the burial Mary anointed the Lord with oil, but we celebrate the symbols of his passion and resurrection in baptism, why are we anointed first with oil, then, after we have celebrated the aforesaid symbols in the bath, again are anointed with oil? And why do we not seem to do these things for us, contrary to those done around the Lord, if indeed the Lord was first anointed with oil and then died? And why also is the anointing of oil not administered in vain for those needing baptism, if indeed the Lord was anointed with oil only for death?

Answer: Since the Church does those things after the death of the one who was buried which it does at the burial, blessed Mary anointed the Lord before death.

Therefore, it is also written, "What she has done," he says, "she has done for my burial, for she has come forward to anoint my body." But the expression "come forward" equally may also mean, "Before the appointed time she has anointed my body."

Therefore nothing happens which is contrary, but what was done around the Lord beforehand happens at the appropriate time for those needing baptism. We are anointed with the ancient oil that we may become "christs" ("anointed ones"), but by an anointing for the memory of the savior Christ. He directed that the anointing of oil be his burial, and he called us to a sharing of his death and glory through a figure in this life, but in reality in the future.

CorpAp 5:220.

43. Tertullian (155–220), *On the Resurrection of the Dead* 8, 3 (210–212?)

The flesh is washed that the soul may be cleaned; the flesh is anointed that the soul may be consecrated; the flesh is signed that the soul may be fortified; the flesh is shaded by the imposition of the hand so that the soul may be illumined with the Spirit; the flesh is fed the body and blood of Christ that the soul may be feasted on God.

CSEL 2:931.

44. Origen (c. 185–253), *Homily on Leviticus* 9

And don't be surprised that this sanctuary is reserved for priests alone. For all whoever have been anointed with the oil of sacred chrism have become priests, as also Peter says to the whole Church: "You are a chosen people, a royal priesthood, a holy nation" (1 Pet 2:9). Therefore you are a "priestly people," and on that account you approach holy things.

GCS 29:417.

45. Cyril of Jerusalem (c. 315–387), *Catechesis* 3, 2–7 (350?)

(Cyril comments on the rituals of initiation; here, on the post-baptismal anointing.)

Just as Christ was truly crucified, buried, and raised again, and you are considered worthy to be crucified, buried and raised with him in likeness by baptism, so too in the matter of anointing, Christ was anointed with the spiritual oil of gladness because he is the author of spiritual joy; and you have been anointed with chrism because you have become fellows and sharers of Christ.

But be sure not to regard the chrism merely as ointment. Just as the bread of the Eucharist after the invocation of the Holy Spirit is no longer just bread, but the body of Christ, so the holy chrism after the invocation is no longer ordinary ointment but Christ's grace, which through the presence of the Holy Spirit instills his divinity into us. It is applied to your forehead and organs of sense with a symbolic meaning; the body is anointed with visible ointment, and the soul is sanctified by the holy, hidden Spirit.

First you were anointed on the forehead so that you might lose the shame which Adam, the first transgressor, everywhere bore with him, and so that you might "with unveiled face behold the glory of the Lord." Next you were anointed on the ears, that you might acquire ears which will hear those divine mysteries of which Isaiah said: "The Lord has given me an ear to hear with." Again, the Lord Jesus in the gospel said: "He who has ears to hear, let him hear." Then you were anointed on the nostrils, so that after receiving the divine chrism you might say: "We are the aroma of Christ to God among those who are being saved." After that you were anointed on the chest, so that "having put on the breast-plate of righteousness, you might stand against the wiles of the devil." Just as Christ after his baptism and visitation by the Holy Spirit went out and successfully wrestled with the enemy, so you also, after your holy baptism and sacramental anointing, put on the armour of the Holy Spirit, confront the power of the enemy, and reduce it saying: "I can do all things in Christ who strengthens me."

Now that you are reckoned worthy of this holy chrism, you are called Christians, and this title you substantiate by your new birth. For before being thought worthy of this grace you did not strictly merit such an address. You were still advancing along the path towards being Christians.

(Cf. SC 126:124f.) *The Awe-Inspiring Rites of Initiation: Baptismal Homilies of the Fourth Century*, trans. Edward Yarnold, S.J., 80–82.

46. Gregory Nazianzen (c. 330–390), *Prayer* 40 (On Holy Baptism) 15

And if you have fortified yourself through baptism, and if you guard against the future with the most beautiful and secure help for you, namely consigning your soul and body with the anointing and the Spirit—like Israel, who once protected the firstborn on that bloody night—what may befall you, and what fortress will be compared to you?

PG 36:377f.

47. Ambrose (334–397), *On the Sacraments* 2:7, 24; 3:2, 8–10 (390?)

Therefore you were immersed, and you came to the priest. What did he say to you? "God the Father almighty," he said, "has given you rebirth out of water and the Holy Spirit and has forgiven you your sins. He himself anoints you into eternal life." See where you have been anointed—into eternal life, he said. Do not prefer this life to that life. For example, if some enemy rises up and wants you to lay aside your faith, if he threatens that someone will wage death, mind what you choose. Do not choose that in which you have not been anointed, but chose that in which you have been anointed, that you may prefer eternal life to temporal life.

There follows the spiritual sign which you heard read today. For after the font there remains that there be a perfection, when the Holy Spirit is poured out at the invocation of the priest, "the Spirit of wisdom and understanding, the Spirit of counsel and strength, the Spirit of knowledge and piety, the Spirit of holy fear—as seven powers of the spirit.

Certainly all powers pertain to the Spirit, but these are as it were cardinal or foundational ones. For what is as foundational as piety, or the knowledge of God, or strength, or the counsel of God, or the fear of God? As the fear of the world is a weakness, so the fear of God is a great strength.

These are the seven powers when you are consigned. For as the holy apostle said, "Since the wisdom of our Lord has many forms," and the wisdom of God has many forms, so the Holy Spirit has many forms, who has diverse and various strengths. For this reason he is also called the "God of strengths," a title befitting the Father, Son, and Holy Spirit. But this is for another discussion at another time.

SC 25:70. 74f.

48. Council of Laodicea, canon 48 (c. 343–381)

Those who have been baptized should be anointed with heavenly chrism after their baptism, and become participants in the kingdom of Christ.

Hefele, Charles Joseph. *Histoire des Conciles*. Trans. a Benedictine. Paris: Letouzey et Ane, Editeurs, 1907. 1:2, 1021.

49. John Chrysostom (c. 344–407), *Homily on Baptism* 2, 22–25 (388?)

Then once you have made this covenant, this renunciation and contract, since you have confessed his sovereignty over you and pronounced the words by which you pledge yourself to Christ, you are now a soldier and have signed on for a spiritual contest. Accordingly the bishop anoints you on the forehead with spiritual chrism, placing a seal on your head and saying: "N. is anointed in the name of the Father, the Son, and the Holy Spirit."

Now the bishop knows that the Enemy is enraged and is sharpening his teeth going around like a roaring lion, seeing that the former victims of his tyranny have suddenly defected. Renouncing him, they have changed their allegiance and publicly enlisted with Christ. It is for this reason that the bishop anoints you on your forehead and marks you with the seal, to make the devil turn away his eyes. He does not dare to look at you directly because he sees the light blazing from your head and blinding his eyes. From that day onwards you will confront him in battle, and this is why the bishop anoints you as athletes of Christ before leading you into the spiritual arena.

Then after this at the appointed hour of the night, he strips you of all your clothes, and as if he were about to lead you into heaven itself by means of these rites, he prepares to anoint your whole body with this spiritual oil so that his unction may armour all your limbs and make them invulnerable to any weapons the Enemy may hurl.

After this anointing he takes you down into the sacred waters, at the same time burying the old nature and raising "the new creature, which is being renewed after the image of the creator (Col 3:10)." Then by the words of the bishop and by his hand the presence of the Holy Spirit flies down upon you and another man comes up out of the font, one washed from all the stain of his sins, who has put off the old garment of sin and is clothed in the royal robe.

Yarnold, 166–168.

50. Augustine (354–430), *On Baptism*, 3:16, 21 (400)

But that the Holy Spirit is said to be given in the catholic Church alone through the imposition of the hand, doubtless our elders wanted this to be understood which the Apostle said, "Because the charity of God has been poured out in our hearts through the Holy Spirit who has been given to us."

For that is the charity which they do not have who were cut off from communion of the catholic Church. Through this, even if they may speak with the tongues of humans and angels, if they may know all sacraments and all wisdom and if they may have all prophecy and all faith so that they would move mountains and distribute all their possessions to the poor and hand over their bodies so that they burn, it profits them nothing.

But one does not have the charity of God who does not love the unity of the Church. Through this the Holy Spirit is understood rightly to be said that he is not received except in the catholic Church.

For neither is the Holy Spirit given only through the imposition of hands when temporal and sensible miracles attest to this, as earlier the Spirit was given for the support of inexperienced faith and for extending the beginnings of the Church.

For who expects this now, that those on whom hands are imposed for receiving the Holy Spirit suddenly begin to speak in tongues? But invisibly and secretly divine charity is understood to be inspired in their hearts because of the bond of peace that they may be able to say, "Because the charity of God has been poured out in our hearts through the Holy Spirit Who has been given to us."

But many are the operations of the Holy Spirit which the same Apostle had mentioned in a certain text when he judged how much they imbued, so he concluded, "But one and the same Spirit works all these things, dividing the properties for each one just as he wills."

Since then the sacrament is one thing, which even Simon the magician was able to have; the operation of the Spirit is another thing, which is accustomed to happen even in evil people, as Saul possessed prophecy; the operation of the same Spirit which only the good are able to have is yet another thing, since just as charity is the end of the law concerning a pure heart and good conscience and a faith not feigned—which the heretics and schismatics may receive—the charity which covers a multitude of sins is a proper gift of catholic unity and peace. Charity is not a gift of unity and peace in all people, because neither do all belong to it, as we will see in its place. Outside of catholic unity, nevertheless, that charity is not able to exist, without which other things, even if they can be recognized and proved, nevertheless are not able to be useful and liberate.

But the imposition of hands is not like baptism, which cannot be repeated. For what else is it but a prayer over a person?

CSEL 51:212-213.

51. Apostolic Constitutions (c. 370–380), 44

When he has baptized in the name of the Father and of the Son and of the Holy Spirit, he anoints them with oil and says, "Lord God, who are unborn and have no lord, the Lord himself of all, who offered the sweet aroma of the knowledge of the gospel among all nations, be present now that this anointing become efficacious in the baptized, where the fragrance of your Christ may remain sure and steadfast, for whom having died they will rise and enjoy life."

Didascalia et Constitutiones apostolorum. Ed. Francis Xavier Funk. 2 vols. Paderborn: Libraria Ferdinandi Schoeningh, 1905. 1:451.

52. Pacianus of Barcelona (+ c. 392), *On Baptism* 6 (c. 370–392)

Christ must be received for one to be born, for as John the apostle says, "However many received him, to them he gave the power to become children of God (John 1:12)." But these things are not able to be completed otherwise unless by the sacrament of the bath and of chrism and of the bishop. For sins are purged by the bath. The Holy Spirit is poured forth by chrism. But we procure them both by the hand and mouth of the bishop: and thus the whole person is reborn and renewed in Christ.

PL 13:1093.

53. Theodoret of Cyrus (c. 393–466), *Explanation of the Song of Songs* 1, 2

If you want to understand more mystically, remember the mystery of holy baptism. In it, those who are initiated, after the renunciation of the Tyrant, and the confession of the King, have been anointed with the chrism of spiritual anointing, as by a sign and a certain royal mark. They receive under that kind of visible anointing the invisible grace of the most holy Spirit.

PG 81:59f.

54. Theodoret, *Interpretation of the Second Letter to the Corinthians* 1, 21-22

"God is the one who confirms us with you in Christ and anoints us. He also signed us and gave the pledge of the Spirit in our hearts." God is the cause of these goods. For he has given us a firm faith in Christ, he has anointed us, and made us worthy by the seal of the most holy Spirit, as if having bestowed this grace on us as a kind of pledge of future goods. Through "pledge" he intimates the magnitude of those things which need to be given to us. For a pledge is a certain small part of the whole.

PG 82:383-386.

55. Pseudo-Dionysius (431–451?), *The Ecclesiastical Hierarchy* 4:3,11

For this reason the oil of anointing bestows the falling of the Holy Spirit on the baptized themselves, since in this way may be signified the coming of the Holy Spirit through the oil of anointing.

PG 3:497f.

56. Eusebius Gallicanus (7th c.) *Homily 29, On Pentecost,* 1–2

(This text has also been attributed to the fifth century Faustus of Riez.)

"In those days," says the Lord, "I will pour my spirit upon all flesh." Let us turn to the riches of the highest goodness. What the imposition of the hand bestows in confirming individual neophytes, the descent of the Holy Spirit gave people then in the world of believers.

But because we said that the imposition of the hand and confirmation may confirm something for the one who has already been reborn in Christ, some may think to themselves: "What does the ministry of confirming benefit me, after the mystery of baptism?"; or: "As far as I can see, we do not receive much from the font, if after the font we need the addition of a new birth."

Let your charity not so consider it, most beloved. As the military order demands, that when the emperor receives someone among the number of soldiers, he not only signals the engagement but also furnishes the fighter with fitting arms, so with the baptized that blessing is a defense. You have given a soldier; give also military aid. What does it benefit if some parents bestow a great ability on a child unless they also take pains to provide a tutor? Thus the Paraclete, the guard of those reborn in Christ, is consoler and tutor. Therefore the divine word says, "Unless the Lord guards the city, in vain do they keep watch who guard it" (Ps 127:1).

Therefore the Holy Spirit, who descends upon the waters of baptism by a salvific falling, bestows on the font a fullness toward innocence, and presents in confirmation an increase for grace. And because in this world we who will be prevailing must walk in every age between invisible enemies and dangers, we are reborn in baptism for life, and we are confirmed after baptism for the strife. In baptism we are washed; after baptism we are strengthened. And although the benefits of rebirth suffice immediately for those about to die, nevertheless the helps of confirmation are necessary for those who will prevail. Rebirth in itself immediately saves those needing to be received in the peace of the blessed age. Confirmation arms and supplies those needing to be preserved for the struggles and battles of this world. But the one who arrives at death after baptism, unstained with acquired innocence, is confirmed by death because one can no longer sin after death.

CChr.SL 101:337f.

57. John Damascene (c. 675–749), *On the Orthodox Faith* 4, 9

(John writes on a variety of issues concerning baptism, including the anointing with oil.)

And therefore oil is administered at baptism, because it signifies our anointing, and makes us "christs." Moreover, it promises us the mercy of God through the Holy Spirit. For also a dove brought a branch of an olive tree to those once beyond all hope who had disembarked safe from the flood.

PG 94:1125.

58. Rabanus Maurus (776 or 784–856), *On the Institution of Clerics* 1,30

The Holy Spirit, the Paraclete is bestowed immediately on the baptized by the bishop through the imposition of the hand, that they may be strengthened through the Holy Spirit for preaching to others the same gift which he bestowed in baptism, given by the grace of eternal life. For the baptized are signed with chrism by the priest on the top of the head, but by the bishop on the forehead, so that in the first anointing the descent of the Holy Spirit upon them is signified, to consecrate the dwelling for God, and that in the second anointing, the sevenfold grace of the same Holy Spirit is declared to come upon people with all fullness of sanctity and knowledge and power.

For then the Holy Spirit himself descends willingly from the Father after the bodies and souls have been cleansed and blessed, that by his visitation he may sanctify and illumine his vessel, and now he comes to people for this, that the sign of faith which they receive on the forehead may make them filled with heavenly gifts, and comforted by his grace to carry on fearlessly and boldly before kings and the powerful of this age, and to preach the name of Christ with a free voice.

It is no wonder if people are anointed twice with the same chrism for receiving the Holy Spirit, since the same Spirit was given twice to the apostles themselves, that is, once on earth when after his resurrection the Lord breathed on them and said, "Receive the Holy Spirit. Whose sins you forgive are forgiven them, and whose sins you retain are retained." And they received him once from the heavens, when after the ascension of the Lord on the day of Pentecost he came upon the apostles in fiery tongues and permitted them to speak in the languages of all nations.

Therefore the Holy Spirit is called the finger of God in the Gospel, and the law was written by the finger of God. Therefore he is called the finger of God, that his creating power may be signified as with the Father and the Son. But as through baptism we die and are reborn in Christ, so we are signed with the Holy Spirit who is the finger of God and the spiritual sign.

It is indeed well fitting that through sacred chrism and through the oil of the olive the grace of the Holy Spirit is bestowed, because in the psalm it was written about Christ the Savior, that God the Father anointed him with the oil of gladness above his companions, and the same concerning us, that he cheers our face with oil. Chrism, ("chrisma" in Greek) is called "unctio" in Latin, from which name Christ is also called, and from it people are sanctified after the bath.

For as in baptism the forgiveness of sins is given for grace, so through anointing the sanctification of the Spirit is applied for glory, and this example was drawn from the first anointing, by which the ancients were accustomed to be anointed for priesthood and kingship. For this reason Aaron and his sons were anointed by Moses after the bath, that they might become priests of the Lord. And Solomon and other kings were anointed by prophets and priests with the horn of oil, that they might hold the governance of the reign. Although it happened to the flesh, it benefits the spirit, as also the very grace of baptism is a visible performance, that we are immersed in water, but the spiritual effect is that we are cleaned from sins.

Therefore let us also observe the very nature of oil, if anything in it may be understood to be pertaining to this signification. For burning oil illumines and medical oil heals, and poured on water it retains its clarity. This may well demonstrate the gift of the Holy Spirit. For he with the flame of charity and the splendor of knowledge illumines souls. He with the balm of his mercy heals the wounds of sinners through grace. He by the mixture of his strength truly lights up the waters of baptism to dispel the darkness of sins. Sacred Scripture also witnesses this, for Paul says, "The charity of God is poured forth in our hearts through the Holy Spirit, who was given to us." And John says, "Those who love their brothers and sisters remain in the light." And he says again, "You have an anointing from the Holy Spirit and you know all things." Clearly the statements of the apostles show that we have the light of charity and knowledge through the anointing of the Holy Spirit.

For the Savior in the Gospel shows that the Holy Spirit is the balm of sinners when through him he gave the apostles the power to forgive sins, "Receive the Holy Spirit, whose sins you forgive are forgiven them," and so forth. And that the grace of the Holy Spirit shines fertilizing the waters of baptism, John implies when he witnesed the Lord himself baptizing in the Holy Spirit, saying, "But the one who sent me to baptize in water said to me, 'The one who baptizes in the Holy Spirit is the one upon whom you will see the Spirit descending and remaining upon him.' "

For the water of baptism may never give birth to children of the light unless first it has been illumined by the gift of the same Holy Spirit, that the same Spirit may marvelously effect in it the spiritual birth of light, who in the beginning with the Father and the Son created water fit for cleansing.

Therefore the Lord washes us from sins in baptism and anoints and consigns us "with the Holy Spirit of the promise," and gave the Spirit as a pledge in our hearts, "who is the pledge of our inheritance for the redemption of his own for the praise of his glory, that we may receive the adoption of children. Because you are children of God," says the Apostle Paul, "he sent the Spirit of his Son into our hearts, crying out 'Abba, Father.' "

For the confirmation of all sanctity and virtue and justice consists in this: It is the forgiveness of all sins; it separates the children of God from the children of the devil. "For those who are led by the Spirit of God are children of God." He himself justifies and illumines the holy ones. He is God, he is the gift of God, for he is given by God. "To each is given the manifestation of the Spirit for usefulness" through him. "To one is given the word of wisdom, to another the word of knowledge according to the same Spirit, to another faith in the same Spirit, to another the grace of health in one Spirit, to another the work of virtues, to another prophecy, to another the discernment of spirits, to another the various languages, to another the interpretation of speeches. But one and the same Spirit does all these things, assigning to each as he wishes. For as there is one body, and many are the members, and all the members of the body although they are many are one body, so also is Christ. For all of us have been baptized in one spirit into one body, whether Jew or Gentile, whether servant or free, and all of us have drunk of one spirit."

For we read in the Gospel that the Holy Spirit is called by the name of water, as the Lord himself was calling and saying, "If any of you thirst, come and drink. Rivers of living water flow from within those who believe in me." This evangelist revealed why he says this, for next he says, "For he was saying this about the Spirit whom those believing in him at received."

But the water of the sacrament is one thing, the water which signifies the Holy Spirit is another. For the water of the sacrament is visible, but the water of the Spirit is invisible. The first washes the body and signifies what is in the soul, but through the second, that is, through the Holy Spirit the soul itself is cleaned.

As also the corporal body washes with water and drinks it, so the spiritual body washes with and feeds on spirit. Therefore the Holy Spirit is called sevenfold because of the gifts which in the fullness of his divinity those who were worthy were promised severally to receive. For he is called the Spirit of wisdom and understanding, the Spirit of counsel and fortitude, the Spirit of knowledge and piety, and the Spirit of fear of the Lord.

PL 107:344-346.

59. Pseudo-Isidore (847-852), *Clement, Letter* 4:79-80

Therefore all must hurry without delay to be reborn for God and then to be consigned by the bishop; that is, to receive the sevenfold grace of the Holy Spirit, because the departure from each one's life is uncertain. For when people have been reborn through water, they are confirmed afterwards by the bishop with the grace of the sevenfold spirit, as was recalled. Otherwise a Christian could never be perfected, nor have a seat among the perfect, unless they will have remained not by necessity but by negligence or voluntarily. This we have received from the blessed apostle Peter, as the other holy apostles directed as the Lord was ordering them.

Decretales Pseudo-Isidorianae et capitula Angilramni. Ed. Paulus Hinschius. Leipzig: Bernhard Tauchnitz, 1863, 63f.

60. Pseudo-Isidore, Melchiades, *Letter to All Bishops of Spain* 2

The Holy Spirit, who descends upon the waters of baptism by a salvific falling, bestows on the font a fullness toward innocence, and presents in confirmation an increase for grace. And because in this world we who will be prevailing must walk in every age between invisible enemies and dangers, we are reborn in baptism for life, and we are confirmed after baptism for the strife. In baptism we are washed; after baptism we are strengthened. And although the benefits of rebirth suffice immediately for those about to die, nevertheless the helps of confirmation are necessary for those who will prevail. Rebirth in itself immediately saves those needing to be received in the peace of the blessed age. Confirmation arms and supplies those needing to be preserved for the struggles and battles of this world. But the one who arrives at death after baptism, unstained with acquired innocence, is confirmed by death because one can no longer sin after death (*cf. #56 above*).

CIC 1:1413. (Gratian, c.2, D.5, de cons.)

61. Pseudo-Isidore, Urban, *Letter to All Christians* 7

All the faithful ought to receive the Holy Spirit after baptism through the impositions of the hand of bishops, so that they may be found full Christians, because when the Holy Spirit is poured forth, the faithful heart is extended toward prudence and perseverance.

CIC 1:1413. (Gratian, c. 1, D.5, de cons.)

62. Peter Lombard (c. 1100–1160), Book of Sentences 4:7,3–4

What is the power of this sacrament.

The power of this sacrament is the gift of the Holy Spirit for strength, who was given in baptism for forgiveness.

Rabanus: "The Paraclete is bestowed on the baptized by a bishop through the imposition of the hand, so that they may be strengthened through the Holy Spirit for preaching to others that which they themselves received in baptism" (*cf. #58 above*).

Pope Urban: "All faithful ought to receive the Holy Spirit after baptism through the imposition of the hand of bishops, that they may be found full Christians" (*cf. #61 above*).

Whether this sacrament is worthier than baptism.

Pope Melchiades: "Know that each is a great sacrament, but one should be held in greater veneration as it is given by superiors" (*cf. #118 above*). There he says the sacrament of confirmation is greater. Probably not for the greater power or usefulness which it confers, but because it is given by more worthy ministers, and occurs on a worthier part of the body, that is the forehead. Or perhaps because it offers a greater increase of strengths, although baptism effects more for forgiveness.

Rabanus seems to intimate this, saying that in the anointing of baptism, "the Holy Spirit descends to consecrate the dwelling for God," but in this event, "his sevenfold grace comes to people with all fullness of sanctity and power" (*cf. #58 above*).

This sacrament ought to be bestowed only by those fasting on those fasting, as also baptism, unless necessity dictates otherwise.

SpicBon 5:278f.

63. Nicholas of Clairvaux (fl. 1145–1151) (Pseudo-Peter Damian), *Sermon 69 on the Dedication of a Church*, 1

Second is the sacrament of confirmation. In baptism the Spirit is given for grace, here it is given for the struggle. There we are cleaned from iniquities, here we are fortified with virtues. Does not the consecrated hand press the oil of sacred chrism on the lintel-forehead of our earthly home?

Nor is just any executor of such a great mystery allowed, but only a bishop, upon whose head the oil of anointing was poured and whose flock is placed under priestly authority. The authority of the ancients bestows the grace of baptism to every human of either sex. But only the person of the bishop assumes its dignity with the sign of confirmation.

Hence it is that the decretal writings and the regulations of the holy Fathers decided that the power of this sacrament should not be separated after baptism, lest that deceitful perverter, from whom no one ever wrenches away a truce on hurting, find us defenseless.

Therefore, having been anointed with the ointment of each dew, healed by this one, comforted by that one, do we descend more securely to each battle? Let not the arms of Goliath deter us, nor his greatness of stature shake us, because with us is the great Lord our God and great is his strength (Ps 146), taking up arms and shield that he might arise to our help (Ps 34).

PL 144:898f.

64. Herveus (Pseudo-Anselm) (+ c. 1150), *On the Second Letter to the Corinthians*, 1

He anointed us as kings and priests, because kings and priests were anointed when they were selected, "and signed us," that is separated us from the faithless by the sign of the cross, which he placed on our foreheads, "and gave the pledge of the Spirit in our hearts," when we received the Holy Spirit through the imposition of hands in pledge of future blessing.

PL 181:1011.

65. Thomas Aquinas (c. 1225–1274), *Summary of Theology 3:72,1*

I respond saying that the sacraments of the new law are ordained for the special effects of grace, and therefore where some special effect of grace occurs, there is ordained a special sacrament. But because sensible and corporal things bear spiritual and intelligible similitude, from these things which are done in corporal life we are able to perceive what exists in the special spiritual life. But it is manifest that in the corporal life there is a certain special perfection, when people attain a mature age and may enact the mature actions of humankind.

For this reason the Apostle Paul says in 1 Corinthians 13, "When I became a man I gave up the things that were of a child." And hence it is also that because of the advance of the generation by which someone receives corporal life, there is an advance of increase, by which someone is led to a mature age. Thus therefore people also receive a spiritual life through baptism, which is a spiritual regeneration. But in confirmation people receive as it were a certain mature age of spiritual life.

For this reason, Pope Melchiades says, "The Holy Spirit who descends upon the waters of baptism in a salvific falling bestows on the font a fullness toward innocence. In confirmation it presents an increase for grace.

In baptism we are reborn for life. After baptism we are strengthened" (*cf.* *#60 above*). And therefore it is clear that confirmation is a special sacrament.

Ed. Roberto Busa. Stuttgart-Bad Cannstatt: Friedrich Frommann Verlag Günther Holzboog KG, 1980. 2:885.

66. Hugues Ripelin (13–14th c.), *On Confirmation*, 2

It arms the soul and the body. It arms the soul through the impression of the character against the defect of timidity; it arms the body through the shield of the cross against the insults of demons. It presents boldness against shame and fear in the confession of the name of Christ. . . . It crowns the fighter: This is noted in the band which binds around the head of the one confirmed.

Hugo Argentinensis. *Compendium totius theologicae veritatis, vii. libris digestum*. Ed. Ioannes de Combis. Lyons: Gulielmus Rouillius, 1579. 520.

67. John Wyclif (c. 1330–1384), *Trialogue* 4,14

Alithia: From this text (Acts 8) it is generally agreed that apostolic confirmation should be added on top of baptism, by which people are baptized, since the apostles did it that way. . . .

Phronesis: I do not see that this sacrament is generally necessary for the salvation of the faithful, nor that those pretending to confirm children confirm them regularly, nor that this sacrament should be reserved especially to the bishops of Caesar.

And further it seems to me that it should be more religious and more fitting in the way of speaking of Scripture to deny that our bishops give the Holy Spirit or confirm another giving of the Holy Spirit, because although such speaking in tongues has as much as disappeared from our teachers, the danger of bad understanding remains and weakens the foundation of this way of speaking.

For this reason it seems to certain people that this light and brief confirmation of bishops with its added solemn rites was therefore introduced by the action of the devil, that people in the faith of the Church may be deluded and neither the solemnity nor necessity of bishops may any longer be believed.

Ed. Gotthardus Lechler. Oxford: Clarendon Press, 1869, 292–294.

68. Council of Florence (1439), 224: *Bull on the Union of Armenians*

The effect of the sacrament is that in it the Holy Spirit is given for strength, as it was given to the apostles on the day of Pentecost, and namely that a Christian may boldly confess the name of Christ. Therefore on the forehead, where the source of shame is, those to be confirmed are anointed, lest they be embarrassed to confess the name of Christ and especially his cross, which is a scandal to the Jews, and foolishness to the Gentiles, according to Paul (1 Cor 1:23). For this reason, those to be confirmed are signed with the sign of the cross.

CFI 1:2, 129.

69. Martin Luther (1483–1546), *On the Babylonian Captivity of the Church (1520)*

But at this time we seek sacraments divinely instituted, among which we find no reason that we should number confirmation. Indeed, for the constitution of a sacrament there is required above all things a word of divine promise, by which faith may be exercised. But we read that Christ promised nothing anywhere about confirmation. . . . This is why it is enough to have confirmation as a certain ecclesiastical rite or sacramental ceremony, similar to other ceremonies of consecrating water and other things.

WA 6:550.

70. Martin Luther, *Which People Are Forbidden to Marry* (1522)

But it is important to avoid the deceitful jugglery of the idol-bishops, confirmation, which has no foundation in the Scriptures. And the bishops only deceive the people with their lies that they will give grace, character, and a mark inside. It is much more the character of the beast (Rev 13).

WA 10,2:266.

71. Martin Luther, *On Married Life* (1522)

I permit you to confirm as long as it is known that God has said nothing about it, and also knows nothing about it, and that what the bishops allege about it is false. They mock our God in saying that it is a sacrament of God when it is merely a human invention.

WA 10,II:282.

72. Martin Luther, *On the Epistle of Paul at the Early Christmas Mass* (1522)

Here you hear, "the water," that is the bath. You hear, "to be born again," that is regeneration and renewal, and "the Spirit," whom here St. Paul interprets as the Holy Spirit. And it is noteworthy here that the Apostle knows nothing of the sacrament of confirmation. For he teaches that the

Holy Spirit is given in baptism, as Christ also teaches that in baptism we become reborn from the Holy Spirit.

We do read in the Acts of the Apostles that the apostles imposed their hand on the heads of the baptized that they might receive the Holy Spirit, which is similar to confirmation. But this happened that they themselves might receive the Holy Spirit in outward signs and would speak in many tongues in order to preach the Gospel. But this happened only for a time and does not continue any more.

WA 10,1,1:117.

73. Henry VIII (1509–1547), *Defense of the Seven Sacraments Against Martin Luther*

That confirmation is a sacrament is shown not only by the testimony of holy doctors and by the faith of the whole Church, but also in the clearest passages of holy Scripture. By the visible sign of the episcopal hand it confers not only grace but also the Spirit of grace himself.

Assertio septem sacramentorum adversus Marti. Lutherum (London: Pyrson, 1521; reprint ed., Ridgewood, N.J.: Gregg Press, 1966), "De confirmatione," pages not numbered.

74. Ulrich Zwingli (1484–1531), *On True and False Religion*

The other sacraments are rather ceremonies. For they initiate nothing in the Church of God. For this reason they are removed to a not undeserved place, for they were not instituted by God that by them we might initiate something in the Church. . . .

Confirmation then takes its origin when people began to baptize infants, since only those who were being established in the combat of life were baptized among the ancients. But what was this? Was the danger of death making people better informed on Christian matters? But the error had been drunk, which thought that baptism washed away sins after faith, and which then, as it was accustomed to being attacked more cruelly, dared also to deny salvation to infants, as if Christ were more cruel than Moses, under whom those who had been circumcised or initiated by oblations were counted among the children of Israel, even if they did not yet imitate Abraham in faith, for they were not able to.

CR 90:761f. 823.

75. John Eck (1486–1543), *Handbook of General Arguments Against Luther and Other Enemies of the Church (1525–1543)*

But because in confirmation there is a sensible sign, having the infallible assistance of the grace of the Holy Spirit, it is therefore a sacrament. . . .

Note that after baptism (in Acts 8 and 19) there was a sensible sign, namely the imposition of hands, in which the grace of the Holy Spirit was conferred, and so it was a sacrament. . . .

When the heretics object that Christ did not institute this sacrament, it must be said that Christ did indeed institute this sacrament—not indeed by demonstrating, but by promising. He says in the last chapter of Luke, "But stay in the city until you are invested with power from above." And in the sixteenth chapter of John, "If I do not go away, the Paraclete will not come to you." . . .

When Christ imposed his hand on the children he either instituted or hinted at this sacrament.

CCath 34:104.106.

76. Philipp Melanchthon (1497–1560), *Apology on the Augsburg Confession* (1531)

If we call the sacraments rites which have the command of God, and to which has been added the promise of grace, it is easy to judge which are properly sacraments. For rites instituted by humans will not be properly called sacraments in this way. For it is not of human authority to promise grace. Therefore signs instituted without the command of God are not certain signs of grace, even if perhaps they teach ignorant people and advise something. Truly therefore baptism, the Lord's Supper, and absolution, which is the sacrament of penance, are sacraments. For these rites have the command of God and the promise of grace which is characteristic of the New Testament. . . .

Confirmation and extreme unction are rites received from the Fathers, which the Church does not require as necessary for salvation, because they do not have the command of God. Therefore it is not useless to distinguish these rites from those above which have the expressed command of God and a clear promise of grace.

CR 27:570.

77. Johannes Gropper (1503–1559), *On the Sacrament of Confirmation* (1543)

For those who come to death immaculate after baptism with their acquired innocence are confirmed by death itself, for they may not sin after death. But now since we have passed the Red Sea and entered the vast desert of this world, before we come to the Promised Land, it is necessary to struggle without ceasing with its internal and external enemies, namely, the flesh, the world, and the devil, whose attack is so great that no one may securely boast that he or she can be in this body of sin without sin, since human desires and the remains of former sin resting within us never cease to produce a rebellion against the spirit. Also the world with all stratagems still fights us, burdened with a mortal body.

Then the infinitely skilled devil as a roaring lion, circles forever seeking whom he may devour, so that whoever are about to begin this wrestling-match may deservedly be gravely terrified, unless in the meanwhile they recognize Christ as their redeemer (who rules the flesh, conquers the world, and throws out the devil, the prince of this world.) He helps us who are wrestling to abandon other remedies prepared against these scoffings, that we may form our strength not in our powers but in him. . . .

In baptism we are reborn as children of God, and we receive the promise of a heavenly inheritance, but in order that we may retain this promise there must be a teacher for the pupils. This is why it did not seem enough to Christ that a renewing spirit be imparted on us in baptism, unless also through the sacrament of confirmation was bestowed a guarding and defending spirit, who is however not another, but the same spirit given in baptism. He is other and only other according to the diverse gifts and charisms of graces. For since he is given in confirmation, he is the Paraclete who is the guard, the consoler, and the teacher for those reborn in Christ.

Enchiridion christianae institutionis in Concilio Prouinciali Coloniensi editum, opus omnibus uerae pietatis cultoribus longe utilissimum. Venice: Ioannes Francesius, 1543. Fol. 59.

78. Council of Trent, *On Confirmation*, 1 (1547)

If people say that confirmation of the baptized is an idle ceremony and not rather a true and proper sacrament, or that once it was nothing other than a kind of catechesis by which those close to adolescence explained the reasoning of their faith before the assembly, let them be accursed.

CT 5:996.

79. John Calvin (1509–1564), *Antidote to the Council of Trent, On Confirmation*, 1 (1547)

Since this is a cloven curse, lest I rest in the first rut, I confess quickly that I am not of the number of those who think the ceremony of confirmation is idle, as it is observed under the Roman papacy (*cf. #78 above*). Rather, I number it among the most deadly tricks of Satan. Let us remember that what they make a sacrament is never entrusted to us in the Scripture, not by this name, not with this rite, not with this meaning.

Now we hear that they are adorning this creation with certain statements. They announce under the name of Pope Melchiades that the spirit is given in baptism toward innocence, and in confirmation for an increase toward grace (*cf. #60 above*). They claim that baptism suffices for those soon about to die, but those who will be prevailing are armed with confirmation that they be able to sustain the struggles.

So a half part of efficacy is lopped off from baptism, as if it were said for nothing that the old person is crucified in baptism, so that we may walk in newness of life (Rom 6:6).

They add besides that, although neither of these two may be completed without the other, confirmation nevertheless should be held in greater veneration than baptism. For there exists a decree of the Council of Orleans that no one should be esteemed a Christian who has not been chrismated by an episcopal anointing (*cf. #19 above*). For their words are worthy only to be furnished to children for sport. A sacrilege so stuffed with execrable blasphemies differs much from an idle ceremony.

Concerning the second part of Trent's decree, what else can I say but that they estimate poorly how little their curses are worth? They are so ready with this vomit that they think black should become white on the spot. This much is true, that in the admiration of the people, or rather in what stupor their mysteries were gawked at up to now, they think that whatever they babble will be followed in the same way. For this reason they have such great confidence. For they would not have dared to submit their absurdities to the judgment of the dullest swineherd if they had not hoped that this scarecrow of a council covered the eyes of all.

CR 35:501f.

80. Johannes Brenz (1499–1570), *On the Sacraments: On Confirmation* (1561)

We do not doubt that at the beginning of the good news revealed and confirmed on the day of Pentecost the apostles conferred by the imposition of hands the wondrous gift of the Holy Spirit on those believing in Christ, that they might speak in different tongues.

And we think it is most useful that children and adolescents be examined in the catechism by the pastors of their Church, and if they will have been piously and rightly formed, they may be approved. But if wrongly, they may be corrected.

But from the personal and temporal deed of the apostles there is no certain mandate of God establishing a general and perpetual sacrament in the Church. And it is horrible to hear that the sacrament of confirmation, which suffragan bishops are accustomed to bestow on children, excels by its dignity the sacrament of baptism. For some have not feared to write this way concerning the sacrament of confirmation. As it is administered (so they say) by greater ministers, that is by bishops, that it may not be completed by lesser ones, so also it must be venerated and held in greater veneration.

For it was divinely conceded to apostles that they confer the gifts of the Holy Spirit on those believing in Christ, by the imposition of hands. But this was not properly understood concerning those private gifts of the Holy Spirit, which were necessary to each for salvation. For the believers receive them through the preaching of the Gospel and through baptism, but this must be understood concerning the public gifts of the Holy Spirit, namely speaking in various tongues and other gifts, which were once necessary for the public confirmation of the Gospel of Christ.

Therefore after the authority of the Gospel was sufficiently confirmed with such miracles, as that miraculous gift of tongues, so also the rite of imposing hands, by which that gift was conferred, was done, that the idle might occupy themselves with this matter. Otherwise a general sacrament will be made for the Church out of a shadow, and the sick will have to be overshadowed, because many found health through the shadow of Peter.

Similarly a general sacrament will be made out of the imposition of handkerchiefs, because others were freed from their diseases when the handkerchiefs of Paul were imposed on them. And there will be laying upon the dead, for Paul raised up an adolescent from death by laying on him.

But it must not be permitted to the pastors of the Churches to have no reason for educating children and youth in truly pious doctrine, but it must be demanded from them, that they diligently teach the catechism.

"Confessio illustrissimi Principis ac Domini, D. Christophori Ducis Wirtembergensis, & Theccensis, Comitis Montebeligardi, &c (1561)." *Corpus et Syntagma Confessionum Fidei quae in diversis regnis et nationibus, ecclesiarum nomine fuerunt authenticé editae: in celeberrimis Conuentibus exhibitae, publicáque auctoritate comprobatae.* Editio Nova. Geneva: Petri Chovet, 1654. 2:110.

81. Diego Andrada (1528–1578), *Orthodox Explanations* (1564)

For when the heretics wish to impose laws for divine wisdom, to define its infinite goodness by certain boundaries, to estimate its most secret plans with a certain norm by their own judgment, let it be that they return to Christ only those benefits received which they judge had been necessary for themselves, but which they do not accept, abominably cast away, spurn, or tread underfoot.

This is indeed openly and plainly perceived in this heavenly divine sacrament of confirmation. The origin and foundation of our salvation are placed in the faith and knowledge of Christ, which both opens an access to the happiness promised us by Christ, and inspires us to every kind of service as if by certain incentives. So great may be the weakness of human nature that the fear of nearby death may easily deprive and cut us down off faith.

Christ Jesus, who keeps watch most kindly over the needs of the human race and establishes his own as sheep among wolves, instituted this divine sacrament and impressed on it the strength and power of his blood, that he may make firm for us the faith conferred in the sacred bath, perfect it, and fasten it down as it were with the deepest roots, where neither the storm of danger nor the breeze of honor may sway minds confirmed and strengthened by this great power of the Holy Spirit, from the course of faith, hope, or fear.

Orthodoxarvm explicationvm libri decem, In quibus omnia feré de religione capita, quae his temporibus ab haereticis in controuersiam vocantur, aperté & dilucidé explicantur; Praesertim contra Martini Kemnicij petulantem audaciam, qui Coloniensem Censuram, quam á uiris societatis Iesu compositam esse ait, uná cum eiusdem sanctissimae societatis uitae ratione, temeré calumniandam suscepit. Venice: Iordanus Ziletus, 1564. Fol. 275.

82. Martin Chemnitz (1522–1586), *Examination of the Council of Trent, On Confirmation,* 3 (1566)

The principal point of this controversy is this, how they speak concerning the efficacy of this confirmation of theirs. And this whole disputation cannot be set forth in a shorter abridgment nor be more rightly understood than if this is considered, that in this doctrine of theirs the antithesis of baptism and confirmation is perpetual, so that whatever effects are attributed to confirmation are by that very fact denied to and drawn away from baptism.

Preuss: 285.

B. IRREPEATABILITY

Even though confirmation quickly separated from baptism, it copied one important feature: it was not to be repeated in life. This became an issue, of course, only after the two rites were separated.

The teaching on this point is fairly uniform. Even Martin Luther, in a pre-Reformation passage, supported the common opinion.

83. Council of Orange, canon 2 (441)

By no means should any minister who accepts the duty of baptizing proceed without chrism, because it is agreed among us to be chrismated once. However, at confirmation, the priest will be reminded about those who were not chrismated in baptism, when some necessity appeared. For among certain ministers of this chrism, it is nothing but a blessing, not to foreshadow anything, but that a repeated chrismation not be held necessary.

CChr.SL 148:78.

84. Council of Terracina (516), canon 6

It has been told us that certain people are being confirmed by the same bishop two, three, or more times, while the bishops do not know it. For this reason it seemed to us that the same confirmation should not be repeated, as baptism is not, because it has been decreed that those baptized or confirmed twice or more should serve not the world but God alone most religiously under the regular or clerical habit.

CIC 1:1414. (Gratian, c. 8, D. 5, de cons.)

85. Pope Gregory II (715–731), *Letter 4 to Boniface* (726)

Concerning one who has been confirmed by a bishop, the repetition of such again must be forbidden.

CIC 1:1415. (Gratian, c. 9, D. 5, de cons.)

86. Peter Lombard (c. 1100–1160), *Book of Sentences 4:7,5*

Whether confirmation may be repeated.
It should not be repeated, as neither baptism nor orders.
Augustine: "For injury must be done to no sacrament." This was thought to happen when what should not be repeated was repeated.
Augustine, Against the Letter of Parmenianus: But whether some or none should be repeated is a question. For concerning baptism and orders, which should not be repeated, Augustine openly says, "Each sacrament is given with a certain consecration—one when a certain person is baptized, another when he is ordained. Therefore in the catholic Church it is not permitted that either be repeated," because "injury must be done to neither." This must undoubtedly also be held regarding confirmation. But concerning the others, whether they are able to or should be repeated, we will examine later.

SpicBon 5:279.

87. Hugh of St. Victor (+1142), *On the Sacraments 2:7,5*

That the imposition of the hand ought not to be repeated, as baptism is not, and that it should be celebrated by those fasting.
Concerning the sacrament of the imposition of hands it is certain that it not be repeated for any reason, as baptism is not; and if it was done accidentally it must be punished with a severe penance.

This has also been established, that the sacrament of the imposition of hands not be given or received except by those fasting; children who receive should be at a mature age, that being pure they may receive the gift of the Holy Spirit. For as baptism, which generally must be celebrated only at two times, namely at Easter and Pentecost, ought to be celebrated by those fasting, so also it is fitting that the gift of the Holy Spirit through the imposition of the hand be celebrated by only those fasting, and by fasting bishops—except for the sick and those in peril of death.

PL 176:461f.

88. Arnaldus of Bonnevaux (Pseudo-Cyprian) (+c. 1156), *On the Washing of the Feet*

For the ecclesiastical rules forbid that baptism be repeated. And no consecrating hand then presumes to again draw near to those once sanctified. No one renews again sacred orders once given, no one anoints or consecrates again things anointed by the sacred oil, no one diminishes the imposition of hands or the ministry of priests, because it would be offensive to the Holy Spirit if one could void what he improves by sanctification, what he establishes and confirms once.

PL 189:1650.

89. Pope Innocent III (1198–1216), Pastoralis (1204)

Beyond this, you wanted us to consider whether a subdeacon who had been taken up for ordination without the laying on of the hand ought to be permitted to serve, and if the sacrament of confirmation should be repeated in one who mistakenly had been anointed not with chrism, but with oil. We have briefly directed a response to your fraternity that in such cases nothing should be repeated, but that should cautiously be supplied which was incautiously omitted.

CIC 1:134. (Gregory IX, Decretal. 1:16, 1)

90. Council of Florence, 224: *Bull on the union of Aremenians* (1439)

Among these sacraments there are three—baptism, confirmation, and orders—which imprint an indelible character on the soul; that is, a certain spritual sign distinct from the rest. Hence they may not be repeated for the same person. But the other four do not imprint a character and admit repetition.

CFI 1:2, 128.

91. Martin Luther (1483–1546), *Little Commentary on the Letter of Blessed Paul the Apostles to the Hebrews*, 6 (1517)

And for this reason it is said by all theologians that the sacraments of baptism and confirmation are not repeatable.

WA 57,III:180.

92. Council of Trent, *On the Sacraments*, canon 1 (1547)

If people say that in three sacraments—namely, baptism, confirmation, and orders—a character, that is a certain spiritual and imperishable sign by which these may not be repeated, is not imprinted on the soul, let them be accursed.

CT 5:995.

93. Robert Bellarmine (1542–1621), *On Sacraments in General* 2,19 (1588)

"A character is imperishable." This is taken up in all noted councils and it is conceded by them all. The reasoning is *a posteriori*, for it states that sacraments which imprint a character cannot be repeated.

Battezzati 3:121.

3

RITUAL MEANS

A. THE MINISTER

The question of the proper minister of confirmation was first asked as the rite was separating from baptism. Bishops generally presided over the initiation rites in the early Church. But as assemblies grew large and bishops grew few, as populations shifted and the Church expanded, it was no longer possible for bishops to preside at the initiation of all at the Easter Vigil. In the West, presbyters, who had already begun celebrating Eucharist in parish churches, also began the ministry of baptism, including a post-baptismal chrismation. But confirmation was reserved for bishops. When presbyters confirmed, it was by way of exception.

The practice generated literature on the dignity of the sacrament and the ranking of ministers, especially in the Middle Ages.

The practice was predictably challenged in the Reformation, as the theology of both confirmation and orders underwent revision.

94. Council of Elvira (305), canons 38 and 77

Travelers abroad or those in an area far from a church may baptize a faithful catechumen placed in the necessity by sickness, if the bath is unbegun and the catechumen is not a bigamist. If the catechumen survives, they lead him or her to the bishop, that the catechumen may profit through the laying on of hands.

If any deacon governing the people baptizes some without the bishop or the presbyter, the bishop will have to perfect them through the blessing. If they leave this world beforehand, under the faith in which they believed, they are able to be justified.

Mansi 2:12, 18.

95. Jerome (331–419), *Dialogue Against the Luciferians* 9 (382)

Indeed I do not deny that this is the custom of the Churches, that the bishop runs around to impose the hand for the invocation of the Holy Spirit, on those who were far from major cities who were baptized by presbyters and deacons.

But what is this that you apply the laws of the Church to a heresy, and let suffer the integrity of your virgin through the brothels of harlots? If a bishop imposes the hand, he imposes on those who were baptized in the correct faith, who believe that in the Father and the Son and the Holy Spirit three persons are one substance.

But when Arius believed nothing else (stop your ears, I beg you who are about to hear, lest you be defiled by the voices of such impiety) but in the Father as the only true God, and in Jesus Christ as the creature Savior, and in the Holy Spirit as the servant of both, how does one who has not yet pursued the forgiveness of sins receive the Holy Spirit from the Church?

Indeed the Holy Spirit inhabits only a clean abode; nor does he become the dweller of that temple which does not have the true faith as its bishop. If at this point you ask why those baptized in the Church do not receive the Holy Spirit, whom we agree is given in true baptism, except through the hands of the bishop, learn that this opinion descends from that authority, that after the ascension of the Lord the Holy Spirit descended on the apostles. And in many places we find the same practice more for the honor of priesthood than for the law of necessity. Otherwise, if the Holy Spirit pours forth only at the prayer of the bishop, they are to be pitied who, having been baptized by presbyters and deacons, died in forts, castles, or in more remote places before they were visited by bishops.

PL 23:172f.

96. Ambrose (334–397), *Commentary on Ephesians* 4, 11-12

(Ambrose explains the functions of various ordained ministries in his Church.)

In Egypt presbyters consign if the bishop is not present. But because succeeding presbyters began to be found unworthy for holding primacy, the opinion was unchanged, which the council had foreseen, that not order but merit may create a bishop, established by the judgment of many priests, lest an unworthy candidate take possession by chance, and be a scandal for many.

PL 17:410.

97. Augustine (354–430), *On Baptism* 5:20 (400)

How does a murderer clean and sanctify water? How does darkness bless oil? But if God is present in the sacraments and in his words, through whomever they are administered, the sacraments of God are everywhere set right, and evil people who profit nothing are everywhere thwarted.

CSEL 51:285.

98. Apostolic Constitutions, 16:2-3 (370–380)

On many other occasions the place of a woman deaconess is necessary. First when women descend to the water of baptism, those descending into the water should be anointed with the oil of anointing by a deaconess. And where a women and especially a deaconess is not found, it is necessary that the one baptizing anoint her who is baptized. But where there is a woman, and especially a deacon, it is not fit for women to be observed by men; except that in the imposition of the hand you may anoint only the head, as priests and kings in Israel were once anointed.

And according to this analogy in the imposition of the hand you may anoint the head of those who receive baptism, whether men or women. And afterwards, when you baptize—whether you arrange to baptize either with deacons or with priests—the deaconess, as we have already said, may anoint women, but a man should pronounce over them the names of invocation of the Deity in the water. And when she who is baptized comes up from the water, the deaconess takes and teaches and instructs her to be an unbreakable figure of baptism in chastity and in sanctity.

Funk, 1:208.210.

99. Council of Carthage II, canon 3 (390)

It is decreed by all the bishops, that the making of chrism and the consecration of young girls may not be done by presbyters. This pleases all, that a presbyter is not permitted to reconcile anyone with the public dismissal.

CChr. SL 149:13-14.

100. Council of Carthage III (c. 398), canon 36

A presbyter may not consecrate virgins if the bishop has not been consulted. But he may never make chrism.

CChr.SL 149:335.

101. Council of Carthage IV, canon 36 (c. 398)

Presbyters who govern Churches throughout dioceses ask for chrism before the solemnity of Easter. They ask not from whatever bishop they please, but from their own, and not through a junior cleric, but either by themselves or through the one in charge of the sanctuary.

CChr.SL 149:347.

102. Pope Innocent I (401–417), *Letter to Decentius of Gubbio* (416)

About consigning neophytes, it is clear that it is not permitted to take place by anyone other than a bishop. For although presbyters are priests, they nevertheless do not possess the pontifical degree.

Not only does ecclesiastical custom demonstrate that this should be owed to bishops alone—either to consign or bestow the paraclete Spirit—but also that reading of the Acts of the Apostles (8:14-17) which asserts that Peter and John had been directed to bestow the Holy Spirit to those already baptized. For presbyters it is permitted to anoint the baptized with chrism when they baptize either without the bishop or while he is present, but not to sign the forehead with the same oil that had been consecrated by a bishop. That is owed to bishops alone when they bestow the Spirit paraclete.

BRHE 58:22, 24.

103. Council of Orange, canon 1 (441)

It is agreed that heretics placed in danger of death, if they desire to become catholics, are signed with chrism and a blessing by presbyters if no bishop is present.

CChr.SL 148:78.

104. Pope Gelasius I (492–496), Letter 9

Nor any less do we prohibit presbyters to extend their limit farther, nor to boldly take on themselves the things reserved to the episcopal degree: not to seize for themselves the faculty of making chrism nor of applying the pontifical consignation. Neither should they presume permission for themselves to supply prayers or sacred actions when a bishop is not present, unless they were perhaps commanded. Nor may they presume to sit within his sight, unless commanded, nor to enact the sacred mysteries.

PL 59:50.

105. Martin of Braga (515–580), *Canons from Synods of the Oriental Fathers*, 52

A presbyter is not premitted to chrismate when the bishop is present.

A presbyter may not sign neophytes when the bishop is present, unless perhaps he had been ordered by the bishop.

PMAAR 12:137.

106. Isidore (560–636), *On the Ecclesiastical Offices* 2, 27, *"On the Imposition of Hands, or Confirmation"*

But because after baptism the Holy Spirit is given through bishops with the imposition of hands, we remember that the apostles had done this in the Acts of the Apostles. For thus it is told, "It happened while Apollo was in Corinth that Paul, having traveled the upper parts, came to Ephesus. There when he had found certain disciples, he said to them, 'In believing, have you received the Holy Spirit?' And they said to him, 'But we have not heard if there is a Holy Spirit.' And he said to them, 'In what were you baptized, then?' And they said, 'In the baptism of John.' And Paul said, 'John baptized people with the baptism of repentance, speaking that they might believe in him who was to come after him, that is, in Jesus Christ.' When they had heard this, they were baptized in the name of the Lord Jesus, and after Paul imposed the hand on them, the Holy Spirit came upon them, and they spoke in tongues and prophecied (Acts 19:1).

Similarly in another place, "But when the apostles who were in Jerusalem had heard that Samaria received the word of God, they sent Peter and John to them. When they came, they prayed for them that they might receive the Holy Spirit, for he had not yet descended on any of them, but they had only been baptized in the name of the Lord Jesus Christ. Then they imposed the hand on them, and they received the Holy Spirit."

Now, we are able to receive the Holy Spirit. We are not able to give him, but, we invoke the Lord that he may be given. But this may happen principally by the one whom I will suggest, as holy Pope Innocent has written (*cf. #102 above*). For he says it is allowed to happen by none other than the bishop, for presbyters, although they are priests, still do not have the pontifical dignity.

Now this pertains to bishops alone, that either they consign or bestow the Spirit Paraclete. Not only does ecclesiastical custom demonstrate this, but also that aforesaid reading of the Acts of the Apostles, which says that Peter and John were directed to bestow the Holy Spirit on those who were already baptized (Acts 8). For presbyters are permitted when they baptize to anoint the baptized with chrism, either without a bishop or when the bishop is present, but not to sign the forehead with the same oil which had been consecrated by a bishop, which is permitted to bishops alone when they bestow the Spirit Paraclete.

PL 83:824-826.

107. Council of Braga I, canon 19 (563)

Also it is agreed that if any presbyter, after this prohibition, dares to bless chrism, or to consecrate a church or an altar, he may be deposed from his office. For even the ancient canons forbade this.

Mansi 9:779.

108. Pope Gregory I (590–604), Epistle 9, book 4 (593)

Presbyters should not presume to sign baptized infants on their foreheads with sacred chrism. But presbyters may anoint the baptized on the breast, so that afterwards bishops may confirm on the forehead.

CIC 1:1399. (Gratian, c. 120, D. 4, de cons.)

109. Pope Gregory I, Epistle 26 to Januarius, book 4 (594)

It has also come to our attention that some people were scandalized that we prohibited presbyters to anoint those who have been baptized with chrism. And indeed we have done this according to the ancient custom of our Church. But if any are troubled at all by this, we concede that where bishops are absent, even presbyters ought to anoint the baptized with chrism on their foreheads.

CIC 1:331. (Gratian, c. 1, C. 1, q. 95)

110. Council of Seville II, canon 7 (619)

For since the common administration of ministries is exceedingly much for those bishops, presbyters know certain things prohibited to themselves by new and ecclesiastical rules—like the consecration of presbyters and deacons and virgins, or the erection, blessing or anointing of an altar. Nor indeed is it allowed for them to consecrate a church or an altar, to bestow the paraclete Spirit through the imposition of hands on the baptized faithful or on converts from heresy, to make chrism, to sign the forehead of the baptized with chrism, and not to publicly reconcile any penitent in the dismissal, nor to send composed epistles to anyone.

Mansi 10:559.

111. Bede (c. 673–735), *Exposition on the Acts of the Apostles* 8:4

"They sent Peter and John to them." Arator explains this beautifully: "Peter often made John his companion because a virgin is pleasing to the Church."

But it must be noted that Philipp who was evangelizing in Samaria was one of the seven; for if he were the apostle he would have been able to impose the hand that they might receive the Holy Spirit. "For this is reserved to bishops alone. For it is permitted to presbyters when they baptize either without the bishop or when the bishop is present to anoint those baptized with chrism; but not to sign the forehead from the same oil which was consecrated by the bishop, which is reserved to bishops alone when they bestow the Spirit paraclete on the baptized (Innocent to Decentius)" (*cf. #102 above*).

CChr.SL 121:39.

112. Alcuin (735–804), *On the Divine Offices* 19

Of this confirmation Pope St. Innocent says it is not permitted to be done by anyone other than the bishop. For although presbyters are priests, they do not have the pontifical degree, and therefore it is reserved for bishops alone, that they consign or bestow the paraclete Spirit, as the reading of the Acts of the Apostles shows, which states that Peter and John were directed to bestow the Holy Spirit on the baptized. But it is permitted to presbyters, either without the bishop or when the bishop is present, when they baptize, to anoint the baptized with chrism, but with that which was consecrated by a bishop, but not to sign the forehead from the same oil which is reserved to bishops alone, when they bestow the paraclete Spirit on the baptized.

PL 101:1220.

113. Amalarius (c. 780–850) Official Book 1:27, 3 and 5

Hence, one of them, the noted doctor Bede, says in his tract on the Acts of the Apostles, "For it is permitted to presbyters either without the bishop, or when the bishop is present, when they baptize, to anoint the baptized with chrism, but with chrism which was consecrated by a bishop; but not to sign the forehead from that same oil which is reserved to bishops alone when they bestow the Spirit paraclete on the baptized" (*cf. #111 above*). . . . . But the bishop neglects the words, "He himself anoints you with the chrism of salvation," as if I am told he is not only able to save, but also to enrich.

StT 139:139.

114. Pope Leo III (795–816), Letter 86

It is indeed not permitted for them to erect altars, nor to consecrate churches or altars, nor to bestow the holy Paraclete Spirit through the imposition of hands on the baptized faithful or those converted from heresy, nor to make chrism, nor to sign the foreheads of the baptized with chrism, nor indeed to publicly reconcile any penitent in the dismissal, nor to send composed letters to any they please.

All these things have been forbidden to suffragan bishops, who are known to be an example and form of the seventy disciples, and to presbyters, who carry the same figure: because although they have consecration, they nevertheless do not have the pontifical degree.

PL 55:1325.1327.

115. Council of Meaux, canon 6 (845)

Bishops should not bestow the Holy Spirit through the imposition of hands unless they fast—except for those sick or in danger of death. As on two occasions, namely Easter and Pentecost, baptism ought to be celebrated by those fasting, so also it is fitting that the bestowal of the Holy Spirit be celebrated by fasting bishops.

CIC 1:1414. (Gratian, c. 7, D., 5, de cons.)

116. Pseudo-Isidore (847–852), Damasus, *On Avoiding the Empty Superstition of the Suffragan Bishops* 19. Letter 3

It is not permitted to the suffragan bishops to consecrate priests, deacons, subdeacons or virgins; to erect, anoint, or consecrate an altar; to dedicate churches; to make chrism; to sign the foreheads of the baptized with chrism; to reconcile anyone publicly in penance; to send composed letters; to bless people; to enter before the bishop in the baptistry or the sanctuary; to baptize or sign an infant when the bishop is present; nor to reconcile a penitent without a rescript of his bishop. . . .

The Acts of the Apostles teaches that bestowing the Holy Spirit is an office proper to apostles and their successors alone, especially since it is shown that none of the seventy disciples (from whom the suffragan bishops in the Church descend) bestowed the gift of the Holy Spirit through the imposition of the hand, as was said above.

Hinschius: 513.

117. Pseudo-Isidore, Eusebius, Letter 3

The sacrament of the imposition of the hand must also be held in great veneration. It can be performed by none other than bishops. It is read and known that it was not enacted at the time of the apostles by others than the apostles themselves. It ought to ever be able to be completed or to happen by those who take their place. If it had been attempted otherwise it would be void and empty, nor would it be at all regarded among the ecclesiastical sacraments.

CIC 1:1413f. (Gratain, c.4, D.5, de cons.)

118. Pseudo-Isidore, Melchiades, *Letter to All Bishops of Spain* 2

Now concerning those things about which you asked that you be informed; namely, whether the sacrament of the imposition of the hand of bishops is greater, or baptism? Know that each is a great sacrament, and as one has been suited for greater ministers, that is for bishops, that it cannot be perfected by lesser ones, so also it must be venerated and held in greater veneration. But these two sacraments are so conjoined that they should never be separated from each another except when death prevents it, and one cannot be perfected without the other.

CIC 1:1413. (Gratian, c. 3, D. 5, de cons.)

119. Council of Worms, canons 2 and 8 (868)

No one except the bishop may presume to make chrism. For to him alone has this dignity been conceded.

Therefore since the administration of the mysteries common to bishops is exceedingly much, they know certain things are prohibited to presbyters by the authority of the old law, and certain things by new and ecclesiastical rules. Therefore the consecration of virgins, and the blessing or anointing of an altar may not be done by presbyters. Similarly it is not permitted for them to consecrate churches, nor to bestow the paraclete Spirit through the imposition of hands, nor to make chrism, nor to sign the forehead of the baptized with chrism, nor indeed to publicly reconcile any penitent in the dismissal. For all these things are known to be illicit to presbyters, for they do not have the honor of the pontificacy. These things are all allowed to bishops by the authority of canons (*cf. #110 above*).

Mansi 15:869. 871.

120. Pseudo-John III (9th c.?)

It has been brought to the apostolic see to exhume and again revive a custom prohibited and utterly eradicated not only by St. Damasus but also by St. Leo, the apostolic fathers, and the synodal authority of all the bishops. This custom, reprehensible and completely ingrown, is that certain suffragan bishops (who were prohibited this both by the fathers of the aforesaid holy apostolic ancestors and by apostolic men, by them or by us, as their decrees witness thus far), advancing beyond their limit (Council of Paris 6, book 1, canon 27), bestow the gift of the Holy Spirit through the imposition of hands, and contrary to law, enact other things which are reserved to bishops alone. . . .

Although the apostles were few, they did not therefore direct any of the seventy, as has already been said, to this perfecting work, but they sent the Apostles Peter and John to bestow the Holy Spirit by the imposition of the hand. Bishops, and not suffragans, carry the succession of the apostles in the Church (*cf. #18 above*). Before their prohibition, suffragan bishops carried the form of the seventy disciples.

PL 72:13-14.

121. Peter Lombard (c. 1100–1160), *Book of Sentences* 4:7, 2

That confirmation may be bestowed by none except bishops.

Pope Eusebius: "The sacrament may not be performed by others than bishops. It may be read that at the time of the apostles it was not enacted by any others than by the apostles themselves. It may not and should not be performed by others than those who take their place. For if the sacrament had been attempted otherwise, it was held void and empty, nor regarded as among the ecclesiastical sacraments" (*cf. #117 above*). *Gregory:* "But it is allowed to presbyters that they touch the baptized on the breast, but not to sign the forehead with chrism." (*cf. #108 above*).

Gregory, however, writes thus to Bishop Januarius: "Word has come to us that certain people have been scandalized that we prohibited presbyters to touch with chrism those whom they have baptized. And we have done this according to the ancient custom of our Church. But if any are troubled at all by this matter, we concede that where the bishops are absent, even presbyters should anoint the baptized with chrism on the foreheads." "But this is determined once only as a concession for the sake of calming scandal" (*cf. #109 above*).

SpicBon 5:277.

122. Hugh of St. Victor (+1142), *On the Sacraments* 2:7,2-3

That the imposition of the hand is celebrated by bishops alone.

The imposition of the hand which is called confirmation as its usual name, by which the Christian is signed with the anointing of chrism through the imposition of the hand, is reserved to bishops alone, the vicars of the apostles, that they may consign the Christian and bestow the Spirit paraclete, as in the primitive Church the apostles alone are seen to have had the power of giving the Holy Spirit through the imposition of hands.

Concerning the practice which Pope Sylvester instituted, that the presbyter may anoint the baptized with chrism on the crown of the head (cf. #153 below).

Among pontifical gestures it is seen that Pope Sylvester established that the presbyter may anoint the baptized on the crown of the head with chrism, on the occasion of death, lest perhaps in the absence of the bishop, and in the difficulty of reaching him, it might happen that the baptized leave this life without the imposition of the hand.

This would indeed be altogether dangerous. Because as in baptism the forgiveness of sins is received, so through the imposition of the hand the Spirit paraclete is given; in the former grace is bestowed for the forgiveness of sins, in the latter grace is given for confirmation. What does it benefit if you are raised up from slipping unless you are also confirmed for standing?

Furthermore this practice must be dreaded, that people dismiss the presence of the bishop through negligence and do not receive the imposition of the hand, lest perhaps they be condemned for it; because they kept from hurrying to it while they were able.

For because of those who were prevented from receiving the sacrament by a moment of time, that anointing of sacred chrism was instituted by which the priest anoints the baptized immediately on the crown of the head, so that in this very action may be shown how much this sacrament is necessary for salvation, since so anxiously are all admonished not to be drawn accidentally from this life without it.

But it is evident that in all the early times the anointing of chrism was done by bishops alone. But it was instituted afterwards that the priest may anoint the baptized on the crown of the head, but the consignation of the forehead is reserved to bishops alone. For the bishop alone is able to consign and anoint the forehead, and to bestow the Holy Spirit.

PL 176:459-461.

123. Alexander of Hales (c. 1186–1245) *Comments on the Sentences in Four Books* 4:7,6

Confirmation is given by greater ministers.

a. It seems that priests may give this sacrament because they may baptize, which is of greater effect; they may perform the sacrament which is greater.

b. Further, simple priests chrismate on the crown of the head, which is the more excellent part; therefore, they may anoint on the forehead.

c. We respond that in the flock of the Lord are certain ones for the sake of whom a battle is fought, and certain ones who fight for themselves or for others. It is necessary for these to have the strengthened grace or the full measure of grace. For this reason it is fitting that the minister for this grace being bestowed by the Lord be superior in the Church to the one through whom it is first given. Since therefore it falls to priests to give the sacraments of penance and baptism, which are for the weak, it pertains to high priests to give the sacrament of confirmation and orders.

Besides, to confirm, to ordain, to bless abbots, and to sanctify churches are works of perfection; and therefore bishops customarily exercise them in the Church.

Concerning the sacrament of confirmation, Jerome, commenting on Mark 1:4 ("John was there baptizing"), says, "What was finished by the bridegroom was begun by the groomsman." For this reason, as catechumens are initiated by simple priests, they are confirmed by bishops.

d. To the other comment it must be said that chrism on the crown of the head signifies the faith to be given in baptism, which is on the crown, that is on the superior part of reason. Hence, Jeremiah 2, 16: "Sons of Memphis have defiled you up to the crown of your head." Chrism on the forehead signifies the boldness of disciples in preaching the name of Christ; hence, in Acts 2:4: "All were filled with the Holy Spirit and they spoke the word with confidence."

Collegium S. Bonaventurae. 15:131f.

124. Durandus Saint-Pourcain (c. 1275–1334), *Four Books of Commentaries on the Theological Sentences of Peter Lombard,* 4:7,4,9

But what the aforesaid opinion embraces must be observed for coming to know the truth, that confirmation is a true sacrament instituted by Christ, and its minister is any priest, as it is from the institution of Christ, although from the restriction of the Church its conferral has been reserved to bishops alone. Then it is easy to say that by the permission of the Pope a simple priest may confirm, because the restriction of the Church establishes only that it is not permitted for a simple priest to confirm, but it could be allowed to him if there were no restriction of the Church.

Venice: Guerraea, 1571. Republ. Ridgewood, N.J.: Gregg Press, 1964, 2:308.

125. Richard Armachanus (Fitzralph) (1300–1360), *Questions of the Armenians* 11, 4

We do not ask what are the decrees of the Roman Church, but what may appear from the sacred evangelical and apostolic Scripture. As is certainly read in Acts 7 that the apostles imposed the hand on baptized people, so you may read in the First Letter to Timothy 4 not to thus neglect the grace which is in you which was given you through the prophet with the imposition of the hand of the presbyter.

It seems in this saying that this act, namely the imposition of the hand that the Holy Spirit may be given, is shown to pertain to the power of the presbyter, which is one with the power of the bishop. For with us these names of presbyter and bishop have the same meaning. Unless you want to set forth according to your meaning against reason and in the face of the testimony of sacred Scripture that only bishops by the name of presbyter ought to be understood there, or in other sayings similar enough to this one. It will appear that this act pertains not only to apostles but also to all presbyters.

Summa Domini Armacani in questionibus Armenorum. Noviter impressa. Ed. Johannes Sudoris. Paris: Jehan Petit, 1512. Fol. lxxxiii.

126. Marsilius of Inghen (1330–1396), *Questions on the Sentences* 4:5,3

The third conclusion: that the pope may entrust to a simple priest the power of confirming. But this is a special privilege. It is proved because he is able to concede by privilege, as he confers orders. Therefore, the pope may concede that one may confirm.

Argentine: Martinus, 1501. Reprint. Frankfurt/Main: Minerva GmbH, 1966. Fol. cccccviii.

127. Thomas (Waldensis) Netter (c. 1377–1430), *On the Sacraments* 2:114, 1

But then I think the accusation must be resolved which Wyclif raised against the power of bishops, that the ability of confirming the faithful by the sacrament lies to them alone. . . . Hence the devoted brother and teacher William in his book published against Wyclif's Trialogue says that he had wiped this error, as also many others, from the nose of Richard Armachanus, in his book 11 on the Questions of the Armenians, chapter 4, where it seems that he holds "what is in the Gospel," and the "apostolic sayings," he says (*cf. #125 above*). But he does not ask how the Roman decrees speak.

Blanciotti 2:664.

128. Gabriel Biel (c. 1420–1495), *Commentary on the Four Books of Sentences* 4:7,1, *"On the Sacrament of Confirmation"*

Why is the anointing of chrism on the head done by a priest after baptism not a sacrament, just as that which may be done on the forehead by a bishop? For that anointing on the crown of the head is not counted among the sacraments of the Church.

It is answered that other anointings—on the breast between the shoulders with the oil of catechumens, and on the crown with chrism—are not properly sacraments, but sacramentals, because they were not instituted by Christ with such great efficaceous signs of grace. But they were instituted by the Church to arrange for receiving or signifying the grace of baptism, and not principally for conferring grace, for the Church cannot institute in that way.

Brescia: Thomas Bozola, 1574. P. 162

129. Council of Florence (1439), 224: *Bull on the Union of Armenians*

Ordinarily the minister is the bishop. And although a simple priest is able to administer the other anointings, only a bishop may confer this one.

It is told concerning apostles alone, whose succession bishops hold, that they gave the Holy Spirit through the imposition of the hand, as a reading of the Acts of the Apostles reveals. For it says that when the apostles who were in Jerusalem heard that Samaria had received the word of God, they sent Peter and John to them. When they arrived, they prayed for them, that they might receive the Holy Spirit, for it had not yet come to any of them. They had only been baptized in the name of the Lord Jesus. Then they imposed the hand on them, and they received the Holy Spirit (Acts 8:14-17).

But in the Church, confirmation is given in place of that imposition of the hand. Nevertheless, it is told that sometimes through the dispensation of the Apostolic See, for a reasonable and quite urgent cause, a simple priest has administered this sacrament of confirmation with chrism made by a bishop.

CFI 1:2, 129.

130. Pope Adrian VI (1522–1523), *Questions about the Sacraments,* "On the sacrament of confirmation" 4, 7 (1522)

Now the principal question must be examined. The opinion seems more probable to me that the bishop alone is the appropriate and proper minister of this sacrament. So what a simple priest does by trying to confirm outside the commission of the pope is nothing.

Sacrae Theologiae peritissimi, Diuinisque & humani Iuris (quod opus ipsum indicat) Consultissimi, Quaestiones de sacramentis in Quartum Sententiarum librum, summa scientia, maxima pietate, nec minus clariss+ per spicuitate discussae, Vnde uti ex limpidissimo fonte, Christianus quisque salutaria sibi haurire possit, post caeteras impressiones castigatius elegantiusque iterum aeditae. Rome: Marcellus, 1522. Reprint. Ridgewood, N.J.: Gregg Press, 1964.

131. Antididagma, *On the administration of the sacrament of Baptism* (1544)

Perhaps someone will wonder why the presbyter anoints the baptized with chrism, since afterwards the bishop anoints chrism on the forehead in confirmation?

The answer: The deeds of the apostolic bishops note that blessed Sylvester established that a presbyter may anoint with chrism the baptized taken up from water on the occasion of the unexpected arrival of death, lest the baptized, due to the absence of the bishop, whom it may be difficult to locate, might leave this life without the imposition of hands. Therefore Sylvester, as he was wishing to prevent such a case for himself, ordained that when the bishop is absent, the baptized are anointed by a presbyter (*cf. #153 below*). But if the bishop is present, they are anointed, communicated, and so forth, by him.

Still that blessed Sylvester wanted nevertheless that after the anointing which the presbyter does on the crown of the head for the sake of preventing a separation, the baptized should also be confirmed afterwards by the bishop with chrism, but on the forehead. But what is remembered about communion at this place was in existence also during the time of Augustine. Such communion of children was taken up by the Church later along with other things, and not without great reasons.

Antididagma, seu Christianae et Catholicae religionis, per Reuer. & illustriss. Dominos Canonicos metropolitanae ecclesiae Coloniensis propugnatio, aduersus librum quendam uniuersis ordinibus, seu statibus dioecesis eiusdem, nuper bonae titulo Reformationis exhibitum, ac postea, mutatis quibusdam Consultoriae deliberationis nomine impressum. Paris: Ioannes Roigny, 1549. Fol. 60.

132. Council of Trent, canon 3 (1547)

If people say that the ordinary minister of holy confirmation is not the bishop alone, but any simple priest, let them be accursed.

CT 5:996.

133. John Calvin (1509–1564), *Antidote to the Council of Trent, On Confirmation*, 3 (1547)

And certainly the horned and mitred asses are worthy of such a privilege (*cf. #132 above*). For what should they do when they are no more fit for fulfilling the episcopal office than pigs are for singing? I do not look askance at them, but let them drag filth of this kind around their taverns, outside the Church of God.

But how, I ask, will they prove that these offices pertain to bishops more than to other priests, unless that it has so pleased questionable authors? For if a reason be demanded from Scripture, there is by everyone's admission no distinction of bishop and presbyter there.

For Paul was ordered to receive the imposition of hands from Ananias, who was one of the disciples (Acts 9:17). If for them confirmation is the imposition of hands, why do they not accuse God of a violated ritual, and therefore a profaned mystery, in which a presbyter mixes indiscriminately with a bishop?

Then what they want has been sanctioned either by a law of God or by human agreement. If the law is of God, why are they not afraid to violate it? For they concede the right of confirming to presbyters extraordinarily. But thundering so for the sake of a human agreement, in whom will they strike fear?

CR 35:502.

134. Martin Chemnitz (1522–1586), *Examination of the Council of Trent, On Confirmation,* 26 (1566)

As the bishops are, so is the ministry they want to have. For because they have cast off the preaching of the Word and the administration of true sacraments from themselves and to inferior others, they invented the smearing of the chrism, laborious and troublesome to the least degree, lest they themselves have nothing to do.

Preuss:298.

B. MATTER AND FORM

The concept that sacraments are composed of matter and form reaches its development in the Middle Ages. The texts are of note since the question of both is still a part of theological discourse. What words best describe the purpose of the sacrament? Does oil symbolize its action better than the imposition of hands?

135. Peter Lombard (c. 1100–1160), *The Book of Sentences* 4:7,1

Concerning confirmation.
Now something must be added concerning the sacrament of confirmation, by what power it is accustomed to be obtained. For the form has been disclosed—namely, the words which the bishop says when he signs the baptized on their foreheads with sacred chrism.

SpicBon 5:276.

136. Alexander of Hales (c. 1186–1245), *Comments on the Sentences in Four Books* 4:24,1

That form of words which is in confirmation, because it was not expressed by the Lord or by the apostles, is not of the substance of the sacrament of confirmation, but only the anointing of chrism on the forehead.

Ed. PP. Collegium S. Bonaventurae. *Bibliotheca Franciscana Scholastica Medii Aevi* 15. Quaracchi, Florence: Typographia Colegii S. Bonaventurae, 1957, 421.

137. Bonaventure (c. 1217–1274), *Commentary on the* Sentences 4:7,2

Christ did not institute confirmation, because those believing after his ascension had to be confirmed. Hence the apostles dispensed neither the matter nor the form but the *res sacramenti* without the form, by the Holy Spirit confirming unmediated, and without the element or the matter, because in giving the Holy Spirit visible signs appeared. And therefore there was no need of the element. But afterwards the successors had to give the Spirit to the instituted rites on the strength of words and invisibly. Therefore it was necessary that a sensible element be instituted.

Therefore this element was instituted as the Holy Spirit was directing, by the church's own leaders. And because Christ had not instituted the element, nor applied the power to it, as he had applied it to the waters in touching his most pure flesh, and as he instituted the element or matter of the Eucharist as bread or wine by giving his body, therefore bishops not being able to consecrate matters for themselves instituted that they be consecrated through a blessing. And therefore the matter of this sacrament ought to be consecrated.

Editio minor. Quaracchi-Florence: Ad Claras Aquas, 1949. 4:154.

138. Thomas Aquinas (c. 1225–1274), *Summary of Theology* 3:72,2

I respond saying that chrism is the appropriate matter of this sacrament. For as it has been said, "in this sacrament the fullness of the Holy Spirit is given for spiritual strength," which coincides with a mature age. Now one begins to communicate one's actions to others, where before one lived as it were individually for oneself.

But the grace of the Holy Spirit is designated in the oil. For this reason one is called to be "christus," anointed with the oil of gladness, because of the fullness of the Holy Spirit which one has. And therefore the oil is suitable for the matter of this sacrament. It is mixed with balsam because of the fragrance of its aroma which returns to others.

For this reason the Apostle Paul says in 2 Corinthians 2, "We are the good aroma of Christ," etc. And although many other things are aromatic, balsam is nonetheless especially taken, because of that which has the aroma of excellence, and because it also grants incorruption. For this reason it is said in Ecclesiastes 24, "My aroma is not as mixed balsam."

Busa 2:885.

139. Thomas (Waldensis) Netter (c. 1377–1430), *On the Sacraments* 2:113,1.4

Wyclif wants to reduce to nothing all kinds of Christian anointings—

not only the sacrament of confirmation, but baptism and orders, too, because Christ was not thus chrismated in his person. . . .

But according to Dionysius, those apostles, inspired to this by God, called that sacrament the "perfection of anointing" (*cf. #12 above*). Therefore, no one who wants to be faithful says that the sacrament of confirmation was conferred by Christ and the apostles without oil through the mere imposition of the hand. For he no less imposes the hand who imposes by anointing.

Doctrinale Antiquitatum Fidei Catholicae Ecclesiae. Ed. Bonaventura Blanciotti. Venice: Antonius Bassanesius, 1757. 2:657. 660.

140. Jean Gerson (1363–1429), *A Theological and Canonical Summary Collected in Six Books,* "On the Sacrament of Confirmation"

The form is such: "I sign you with the sign of the cross, I confirm you with the chrism of salvation. In the name of the Father and of the Son, and of the Holy Spirit."

Venice: Dominicus Nicolinus, 1587. Fol. 127.

141. Gabriel Biel (c. 1420–1495) *Commentary on the Four Books of Sentences,* 4:7,1

It is said that words of producing are fixed, as when the form of this sacrament is mentioned, which is, "I sign you with the sign of the cross. I confirm you with the chrism of salvation, in the name of the Father and of the Son, and of the Holy Spirit. Amen." . . .

But in place of the words "I sign," some say, "I consign," (as Pierre La Palud and others), and in place of the word "salvation" some same "sanctification." And it does not matter, because these words have the same meaning.

Bozola:157.

142. Council of Florence, 224: *Bull on the Union of Armenians* (1439)

The second sacrament is confirmation, whose matter is chrism blessed by a bishop. It is made from oil which consciously signifies excellence, and balsam, which signifies the aroma of good character. And the form is, "I sign you with the sign of the cross, and I confirm you with the chrism of salvation. In the name of the Father and of the Son, and of the Holy Spirit."

CFI 1:2, 128f.

143. Cajetan (1469–1534), *Summary of Theology* 3:72,2

For this reason we understand that the mixture of oil and balsam (which we are accustomed to call chrism) is the normal matter of confirmation by necessity of the precept, and not by necessity of the sacrament.

Tertia Pars Summae Sacrae Theologiae Sancti Thomae Aquinatis, Doctoris Angelici. Lyons: Haeredes Iacobi Iuntae, 1558. 4:333.

144. Franciscus Victoria (c. 1485–1546), *On the Sacrament of Confirmation*

But balsam is necessary in the matter of confirmation by necessity of the precept. . . . And from the rite of the church. But it is not necessary by necessity of the sacrament, for balsam is only in Syria, the land of the pagans, and may be found with difficulty. And it does not seem that God would want that such difficult matter be the matter of a sacrament. Therefore it is not necessary concerning the essence of the sacrament, as water is not in the consecration of the blood.

Summa sacramentorum ecclesiae. Ed. Marcus Antonius. Venice: Ioannes de Albertis, 1609. Fol. 31.

145. Dominic Soto (1495–1560), *On the Sacrament of Confirmation* 4:7,1,2

And Cajetain on this article says that although balsam is necessary by necessity of precept it is not so by necessity of the sacrament. Therefore those who do not apply it sin mortally, but confect the sacrament. And although I fear I reject the opinion commonly held everywhere, nevertheless since the contrary has not up to now been universally defined by the church, I confess that this opinion has always pleased me, nor may it displease at all.

Commentariorvm Fratris Dominici Soto in qvartum sententiarvm. Ed. Caesarea Maiestatus. Venice: Hieronymus Zenarius, 1584, 1:359.

146. John Calvin (1509–1564), *Commentary on the Letter to the Hebrews* (1549), 6

But the children of the faithful were baptized as infants, because they had been adopted from the womb, and were belonging to the body of the Church by right of the promise. But when the time of infancy had been completed, after they had been instructed in the faith, they were also offering themselves for catechesis, which in those cases was later than baptism. But another symbol was then used, namely the imposition of hands.

This one passage abundantly witnesses that the origin of this ceremony flowed from the apostles. Afterwards it was turned into a superstition, as the world almost always degenerates from the best institutions into corruptions. . . . For this reason the pure institution ought to be retained today, while the superstition ought to be removed.

CR 83:69.

147. Martin Chemnitz (1522–1586), *Examination of the Council of Trent, On Confirmation,* 13 (1566)

But what about the form of confirmation? ("I sign you, etc.") Can it be proved from Scripture either that Christ instituted it or that the apostles used that form of the words? . . .

And so it happens that that form is not the same among the Pontificals themselves. For Gabriel says some say "the chrism of salvation," others "the chrism of sanctification" (*cf. #141 above*). Gerson has this form, "I confirm you with the sign of the cross and chrism" (*cf. #140 above*).

Preuss:289f.

148. Robert Bellarmine (1542–1621), *On the Sacrament of Confirmation* 8, 10 (1588)

Therefore the catholics teach by common consent that the remote matter of this sacrament is oil mixed with balsam and consecrated by a bishop, but the proximate matter, which is properly another part of the sacrament, is the anointing from the aforesaid oil on the forehead, applied in the form or figure of a cross.

The form of this sacrament are these words, "I sign you with the sign of the cross and I confirm you with the chrism of salvation in the name of the Father, and of the Son, and of the Holy Spirit." It may not be doubted that this is an appropriate form, since it clearly explains both the principal cause, which is the Holy Trinity, and the ministerial cause, which is he who offers these words, and also the effect of the sacrament, which is to make a soldier of Christ by signing one with the cross and to strengthen and to arm by confirming with chrism. . . .

Not all these words are found among the ancient authors, and in this order, but the same sense is found and this is enough.

Battezzati 3:222. 228.

C. CHRISM

Chrism has always possessed a certain mystique. Traced to usage in the Hebrew Scriptures, it was adopted for Christian rituals as well.

Councils, theologians, and story-tellers all regarded it with great reverence.

Still, the ritual for blessing chrism provoked discussion during the Reformation. Because of the gesture accompanying the coming of the Holy Spirit in the Acts of the Apostles, the sign of imposing hands replaced the sign of chrism in the Reformers' adaptation of Roman confirmation.

149. Theophilus of Antioch, To Autolycus 1, 12 (c. 180)

Concerning the way you mock me in calling me "Christian," you don't know what you are saying. First, that which is anointed ("christ-ened") is pleasant, useful, and deserves no ridicule. Can a boat be used, can it be safe before it has been anointed? Can a tower, or a house, possess a beautiful appearance and offer good usage until they have been anointed? Does not one who enters into this life, or who goes to fight, receive the anointing of oil? What work of art, what adornment can delight the eye without being anointed and rendered brilliant? Finally, the air and all the land below the heavens are so to speak "anointed" by light and wind. Do you not want to receive the oil of divine anointing? For us, this is the explanation of our name of Christian: We are anointed by the oil of God.

SC20:84.

150. Council of Nicaea, canon 69 (Arabic) (325)

If any of the faithful invokes the law against a woman unfaithful because of fornication, or a faithful woman against an unfaithful man, and if they withdraw from the faith for this reason, their penance is to stand for a period of three years at the door of the temple in sackcloth and ashes.

After this time is completed they may enter into the Church for prayer. But for a period of one year let them stand in the corner of the Church separated from the others. It is not permitted to greet them nor to share communion with them.

However, when the year is finished, the priest ought to bless water and oil, not as it is blessed in baptism, nor as chrism is blessed, but as the oil of the sick, and as water is blessed for cleansing the impurity of those who eat carrion. And thus the priest ought to bless them and to sprinkle them with this water. They themselves ought to feel remorse, and be cleaned, and their sin is forgiven by praying for themselves. A careful examination must be made of them, and then will communion be given. The synod may excommunicate those who are not fit.

Mansi 2:976.

151. Council of Rome, canon 5 (c. 333)

Sylvester the bishop of the city of Rome established with a clear voice that no presbyter may make chrism, saying that Christ will be called by chrism.

PL 8:835.

152. Optatus of Milevis (fl. 365), *Against Parmenianus*

(This anecdote relates how highly chrism was regarded by the faithful.)

And an enormous deed, which may seem unimportant to you, was undertaken, that your bishops mentioned above violated every sacrosanct thing. They ordered the eucharist to be scattered to dogs, not without a sign of divine judgment; for the same dogs, on fire with rabies, lacerated their own masters like strangers and enemies—like thieves, criminals of the holy Body—with tooth as the avenger. They also threw the jar of chrism through the window to break it, and although the toss helped the fall, an angelic hand was not absent. It directed the jar with spiritual support. The jar was unable to feel the fall. With God as defender, it landed unharmed among rocks.

CSEL 26:53f.

153. Pope Damasus I (366–384), *Life of Sylvester* (382?)

In these days a council was held with Sylvester's consent in Nicaea Bithynia. Three hundred eighteen catholic bishops gathered, who set forth an entire, holy, catholic, and immaculate faith. . . .

And in the city of Rome he gathered with the advice of Augustus two hundred seventy-seven bishops. . . . He also established that chrism be made by a bishop. And he conferred the privilege to bishops that they consign the baptized because of heretical persuasion. He also established this, that a presbyter may anoint with chrism the baptized taken up from water, on the circumstance of the approach of death (*cf. #151 above*).

"Decreta Sylvestri Papae Primi." COGP 1:Fol. cxxxvi.

154. Council of Toledo I, canon 20 (398)

Although almost everywhere it is held that no one may make chrism but a bishop, nevertheless, since in some places or provinces presbyters are said to make chrism, it is agreed from this day that no one else but the bishop may make chrism and send it throughout the diocese. Thus in individual churches deacons or subdeacons are appointed for the bishop before the day of Easter, that chrism made by the bishop, destined for the day of Easter, may appear.

Certainly it is permitted for a bishop to make chrism at any time; but without the knowledge of a bishop practically nothing should be done. But it is established that when the bishop is absent, a deacon may not use chrism, but a presbyter may. But if the bishop is present, the presbyter may use it if this has been ordered by the bishop himself. The archdeacon always bears in mind a regulation of this kind. It must be mentioned whether bishops are present or absent, that bishops may keep it, and presbyters not abandon it.

Mansi 3:1002.

155. Augustine (354–430), Interpretations of the Psalms 26:2,2 (392–416?)

"A Psalm of David before he was anointed." . . . He alone was then anointed king and priest. . . . An anointing befits all Christians. . . . It appears that we are the body of Christ because we are all anointed; and in that body we are all both of Christ and Christ, because in a certain way the whole Christ is head and body. This anointing perfects us spiritually in that life which is promised us. But this is the voice of desiring that life; it is a certain voice of desiring the grace of God which is made perfect in us in the end; therefore the psalm is called, "before he was anointed." For we are anointed only in the sacrament, and by the sacrament itself is prefigured what we will be. And I do not know what ineffable future we ought to desire, and what to yearn for in sacrament, that we may rejoice in that reality which is presaged by the sacrament.

CChr.SL 38:154f.

156. Augustine, Tract on the Gospel of John 118, 5 (413–418?)

What is the sign of Christ that everyone knows but the cross of Christ? Unless this sign is administered either on the foreheads of believers, or on that water from which they are reborn, or on the oil by which they are anointed with chrism, or on the sacrifice by which they are nourished— none of those is accomplished correctly.

CChr.SL 36:657.

157. Augustine, *On the First Epistle of John, to Parthos* 3, 5 (413–418?)

"And you have anointing from the Holy One, that you may be manifested to yourselves." The spiritual anointing is the Holy Spirit himself, whose sacrament is in the visible anointing. He teaches that all who have this anointing of Christ know what is evil and good. Nor do they need to be taught, because the anointing itself teaches them.

SC 75:194.

158. Council of Vaison-la-Romaine, canon 3 (442)

Throughout each area, as the solemnity of Easter draws near, presbyters or ministers may request chrism each year not as they may please from neighboring bishops, but from their own bishop. Nor should they request it by whatever ecclesiastic, but if as a necessity or the ministers are occupied, by a subdeacon. For it is not honorable to entrust the highest things to lower ministers. The best is that the one who will be using the chrism in ministering picks it up himself. If something impedes him, at least the one whose office it is to arrange the sacristy and to clean up the holy things should do so.

CChr.SL 148:97.

159. Council of Tours, chapter 9 (461)

Moreover this must also be observed in every way, that holy chrism and consecrated oil always be kept locked, lest some infidel or unclean person touch that by which we are incorporated to Christ, by which all faithful are sanctified, and by which kings and priests are anointed. Or lest some scoundrel steal it to overthrow the judgment of God. We have learned this from experience.

Mansi 7:949.

160. Pseudo-Dionysius (431–451), *The Ecclesiastical Hierarchy* 4:3,4. 4:3,12

We also say that the composition of chrism is composed from most fragrant materials, of which those who are sharers are refreshed with a most sweet aroma by reason of their participation.

Therefore if we say "the mystery of anointing," we also say "the mystery of Christ." But we say the mystery of the consecration of anointing, just as if someone says, "the mystery of the consecration of God."

PG 3:493f. 499f.

161. Martin of Braga (515–580), *Canons from Synods of the Oriental Fathers*, 51

On making chrism.

It is permitted that bishops make chrism at any time and send it throughout their dioceses, so that a deacon or subdeacon from individual churches

may be sent for the bishop to distribute chrism before Easter day.
PMAAR 12:137.

162. Isidore (560–636), On the Ecclesiastical Offices 1:29, 2; 2:26

Hence it is that on this same day (Holy Thursday), the altar and the walls and floors of the church are washed, and the vessels which were consecrated for the Lord are purified. On this day in the same manner holy chrism is also made, because two days before Passover Mary is said to have anointed the head and feet of the Lord with oil. For which reason the Lord also said to his disciples, "Know that after two days it will be Passover and the Son of Man will be betrayed that he may be crucified (Matt 26).". . .

First Moses in the Book of Exodus arranged and made the anointing of chrism, by which Aaron and his sons were anointed first as a witness of priesthood and sanctity (Exod 30), as God commanded. Then kings were also sanctified by the same chrism, by which they are also called "anointed ones" ("christs"), as it is written, "Do not touch my anointed ones (Ps 104:15). And the mystical anointing by which Christ was prefigured was at that time only for kings and priests. For this reason his name itself is called by chrism.

But after our Lord was anointed the true king and eternal priest by God the Father with a heavenly and mystical anointing, now not only bishops and kings but the whole Church is consecrated by the anointing of chrism, because it is a member of the eternal king and priest. Therefore because we are a priestly and royal people, we are thus anointed after the bath, as we are reckoned by the name of Christ (1 Pet 2:9).

PL 83:764. 823f.

163. Council of Braga III, canon 4 (572)

It is agreed that nothing further be demanded for a little balsam, which when blessed is given throughout the Churches for the sake of the sacrament of baptism. Individuals usually demand payment for it. Let us not seem to damnably put up for sale that which is consecrated for the salvation of souls through the invocation of the Holy Spirit, as Simon the magician bartered for the gift of God with money (Acts 8:19)

Mansi 9: 839.

164. Council of Toledo VIII, canon 7 (653)

. . . Not undeservedly does the summit of episcopal eminence survey the greatest of all sacred ministries, which other priests are prohibited from exercising; namely, the consecration of churches of God, the blessing of chrism, and the institution of sacred orders. . . .

But people do not seek to eradicate the holy mixed chrism and the honor of the altar. So also the reverence of the honored saints, which is held equal and partner to these, on whatever occasion has come, will remain unchanged in all ways. . . .

Mansi 10:1217f.

165. Bede (c. 673–735), *Explanation of the Gospel of Luke* 6:22, 39

"And having left, he went out to the Mount of Olives according to his custom; and the disciples followed him." To be betrayed by a disciple, the Lord went to the place of customary solitude where he might most easily be discovered. Where therefore are those who claim he feared death or was crucified unwillingly?

And beautifully he led out his disciples to the Mount of Olives, initiated with the mysteries of his body and blood, that he might designate all those baptized in his death to be confirmed with the most noble chrism of the Holy Spirit. Then they might say with the psalmist, "The light of your face, Lord, has been signed upon us; you have given joy in my heart." And this may appropriately be added concerning them, "His wines and oils have been multiplied in the season of grain."

CChr.SL 120:385.

166. Bede, *On the Song of Songs*

The vines of Engedi are also remembered. For also as we have already said, balsam grows in the vines of Engedi, which is usually mixed with olive oil in the making of chrism, and consecrated with the episcopal blessing, so that all the faithful may be signed in this anointing with the imposition of the priestly hand, by which the Holy Spirit is received, and by which the Lord's altar (when it is dedicated) and other things which ought to be sanctified are anointed.

CChr.SL:206.

167. Alcuin (735–804), *On the Divine Offices* 16-17

Concerning Holy Thursday.
Today chrism is made or consecrated. For this reason Christ, that is the anointed one, is named for chrism. Moses first arranged for this anointing in the Book of Exodus as the Lord commanded. By it Aaron and his sons were first anointed as a witness of priesthood and sanctity. Then kings were also consecrated by the same chrism. For this reason they are also called

"Christs" as in the passage, "Do not touch my anointed ones (Christos)" (Ps 104:15).

And at that time the mystical anointing was only on kings and priests. But after our Lord was anointed true king and eternal priest by God the heavenly Father by this mystic ointment, now not only kings and bishops, but the whole Church is consecrated by the anointing of chrism because it is a member of the eternal king and priest. For it is made from the most pure oil and the best balsam.

Because we are a royal and priestly people, therefore we are anointed after the bath, so that we may be reckoned by the name of Christ. For the chrismal anointing sanctifies those now living from the dead. And therefore it is made on the fifth day, because Christ is said to have come to us in the fifth age of the world, or because two days before Passover Mary anointed the head and feet of the Lord. . . .

On the same day chrism is made: at the end of Mass before "through whom you, Lord, create all these things forever good," chrism is lifted from the jars which the people offer, and as the Pope so all the presbyters bless it. Then the exorcism of oil follows.

PL 101:1205f.

168. Rabanus Maurus (776 or 784–856), *On the Institution of Clerics* 2,36

On the Day of the Lord's Supper holy chrism is also made, because two days before the Passover, Mary is said to have anointed the head and feet of the Lord with oil.

PL 107:347.

169. Amalarius (c. 780–850), *Official Book* 1:12, 26.28

When it is offered by the people it is a simple liquid; through the blessing of priests it is changed into a sacrament. This administration signifies that earthly administration ought to be present for the spiritual. . . .

First I wish to speak to that which says, "He breathes three times on the jar (of chrism)." Breath comes from interior and secret places and proceeds to the public, and it is called the spirit.

StT 139:75f.

170. Pseudo-Isidore (847–852), *Fabian, Decree: Letter to All Oriental Bishops*

On that day, the Lord Jesus, after he had supped with his disciples and washed their feet, as our predecessors received from the holy apostles and passed on to us, he taught them to make chrism; for that washing of our feet signifies baptism, when it is perfected and confirmed with the anointing of holy chrism. For as the solemnity of this day must be celebrated each year, so the making of that holy chrism must be done each year, renewed from year to year, and handed on to the faithful.

Hinschius: 160f.

171. Rupert of Deutz (c. 1075–1129), *Book on the Divine Offices* 5, 17

And you may ask why the consecration itself of chrism was not delayed, so that from Holy Thursday up to Vespers of Saturday at which hour chrism must be used, we are free from the solemnities of the Mass. But it is the custom that chrism itself be consecrated only at the solemnity of the Mass in that place where we receive the sign of peace. And before these things reason demands that baptism be celebrated on this Holy Saturday, as must be said at its place, that is at the great office of Holy Saturday. Therefore the consecration of chrism should not and may not be delayed.

CChr.CM 7:171.

172. Bernard (1090–1153), *Life of St. Malachy* 4, 8

(Bernard tells of miracles which occurred under the episcopacy of Malachy.)

He cured a boy seized mentally among those whom they call lunatics, while confirming him with the sacred ointment. This was so noted and certain that he thereupon appointed him the porter of his house, and the same boy lived unimpaired in that office up to adulthood.

Rome: Editiones Cistercienses, 1963. 3:317.

173. Arnaldus of Bonnevaux (Pseudo-Cyprian) (+ c. 1156) *On the Anointing of Chrism and other Sacraments*

Today in the Church with the other anointings for sanctifying the people of acquisition for the participation of dignity and of name, sacred chrism is made, in which balsam mixed with oil expresses the unity of royal and priestly glory. Oil was divinely instituted for initiating those dignities. . . .

The whole contents of the temple were carried to Assyria. For neither was it fitting that the Christian religion, preoccupied with visible ornaments, be seduced with idols. But the very destruction of the tabernacle and the ruin of the temple, and the holy things removed in plundering, intimate the stability of a more excellent glory. The sacraments remaining forever instruct their worshippers toward the consideration of invisible things. . . .

This anointing was not instituted for treating bodies, because, after the elements have been sanctified, now their own nature does not offer the effect, but divine strength works more powerfully. Truth is present to the sign, and spirit to the sacrament. . . .

From the service of this anointing both wisdom and understanding are divinely given to us, counsel and heavenly fortitude fall from heaven, knowledge and piety and fear are poured forth through supernal inspirations. Anointed with this oil, we contend with spiritual enemies.

PL 189:1653-1655.

174. Pope Innocent III (1198–1216), *"When He Had Come"* 2 (1204)

To produce an exterior and visible anointing, oil which is called "of catechumens" or "of the sick" is blessed, and chrism is made, which comes from oil and balsam in a mystic ratio. . . . The imposition of the hand is represented by the chrismation of the forehead. It is called "confirmation" by another name, because through it the Holy Spirit is given for growth and strength. For this reason, although a simple priest or presbyter may produce other oils, only the high priest, that is the bishop, ought to confer this one, because it is told concerning the apostles alone, whose successors are the bishops, that they gave the Holy Spirit through the imposition of the hand, as a reading of the Acts of the Apostles shows.

CIC 2:132f. (Gregory IX, Decretal. 1:15, 7-8)

175. Thomas Aquinas (c. 1225–1274), *Summary of Theology*, 3:72,3

I respond saying that the whole sanctification of the sacraments is derived from Christ, as has been said above. But it must be considered that Christ used certain sacraments having corporal matter, namely baptism and also eucharist, and therefore from that very use of Christ, the matters of these sacraments received what was appropriate for the accomplishment of the sacrament.

For this reason Chrysostom says that the waters of baptism would never be able to purge the sins of believers if they had not been sanctified by the touch of the Lord's body. "And similarly, the Lord himself, taking bread, blessed it, and similarly the cup," as Matthew 26 and Luke 22 say.

And because of this, it is not from the necessity of those sacraments that the matter be blessed first, because the blessing of Christ suffices. But if that blessing is applied, it pertains to the solemnity of the sacrament, not to necessity. But Christ did not use visible anointings, lest harm happen to the invisible anointing by which he was anointed before his companions. And therefore chrism is blessed just as holy oil and the oil of the sick are blessed before they are applied for the use of the sacrament.

Busa: 2:886.

176. William Duranti (c. 1230–1296), *Order for Holy Thursday* 3:75-82

Another blessing which some say is this: "Lord, Pro-creator, who through your servant Moses ordered that the sanctification of anointing come to the creation of all through the mixing of aromatic herbs, we humbly ask your mercy that you may pour forth the fullness of sanctification onto this ointment, which the root produces from its sprout, by lavishing spiritual grace. Let it be for us, Lord, the joyful wine of faith; let it be a perpetual chrism of priestly anointing; let it be most worthy for a heavenly banner by its application, that those reborn by sacred baptism and anointed with this oil, may obtain the fullest blessing of bodies and souls, and be perpetually fulfilled when the blessed ministry of faith has been conferred. Through Christ our Lord." All respond, "Amen."

Then over the dish or in some other small vessel, let him mix and make the balsam with a bit of oil taken up from the jar, saying in this mingling,

"Let us ask our almighty God, who inseparably joined the incomprehensible divinity of his own coeternal Son with the truly wondrous disposition of humanity, and, as the grace of the Holy Spirit was helping, anointed him with the oil of gladness before his companions, that humanity, lost by the deceit of the devil, consisting of twin and individual matter, may perpetually be restored from which deceit he had forfeited his heredity, so that he may bless with the perfection of the Holy Trinity these liquids created from diverse species of creatures, and in blessing may sanctify and grant that once mixed they may become one, and whoever will have been anointed from it exteriorly, may thus be anointed interiorly, that devoid of all sordidness of corporal matter, humanity may rejoice at becoming a sharer in the heavenly reign. Through the same Christ. In the unity." All respond, "Amen."

Now, what had been mixed in a small vessel earlier is mixed again with the oil in the jar, prepared for chrism, while the bishop says, "May this mixture of liquids become for all anointed from it a kindness and a safeguard of salvation for ever. Amen."

Then, before chrism may be blessed, the bishop blows evenly three times in the form of a cross from his mouth to this stirred-up jar. And similarly all the priests blow in turn, to whom the jar is brought by order of the archdeacon.

When this has been done, after the jar itself has been placed upon the table, the bishop stands, and with a slow voice, as if reading a lesson, begins fully this chrismal exorcism: The Exorcism of the chrismal oil. "I exorcize you, creature of oil, through God the almighty Father who made heaven and earth. . . . Through Jesus Christ his son our Lord, who lives and reigns with him as God in the unity of the Holy Spirit."

Then he says in a medium voice, with hands joined before his heart, "For ever and ever. . ." The preface follows: "It is truly right. . . . We ask you, therefore, Lord, holy Father, almighty eternal God, through the same Jesus Christ your Son our Lord, that you deign to sanctify with your blessing the fat of this creature, and to mix with it the strength of the Holy Spirit, while the power of your Christ assists, by whose holy name chrism receives its name, by which you anointed priests, kings, prophets, and martyrs, that you may confirm the creature of chrism into the sacrament of perfect salvation and life for those being renewed by baptism of the spiritual bath. Then after the sanctification of oil has been poured out, and the corruption of the first birth has been destroyed, the innocent second temple of each acceptable life may emit a scent, that having filled the second sacrament of your constitution with royal, priestly, and prophetic honor, they are dressed in the garment of uncorrupted service, so that it may be the chrism of salvation for those who were reborn from water and the Holy Spirit, and that you may make them sharers of eternal life and companions of heavenly glory. . . . Amen."

When the preface is done, the bishop greets the pure chrism three times, or the jar without the veil, saying three times, always by bending to it, "Hail, holy chrism!" And finally he kisses the jar. Also the twelve priests who have joined him do the same in turn, to whom the jar is brought by order of the archdeacon, veiled, however, that it may be seen by none of them. When this is completed, the jar is placed on a side table.

StT 88:577-579. StT 227:74f.

177. Council of Trent, canon 2 (1547)

If people say that those are injurious to the Holy Spirit who attribute any strength to the sacred chrism of confirmation, let them be accursed.

CT 5:996.

178. John Calvin (1509–1564) *Antidote to the Council of Trent, On Confirmation,* 2 (1547)

The question is whether by the decision of humans oil receives a new and secret power of the Spirit as soon as it will have pleased them that it be called chrism. For there is no one who makes mention of oil—not from the ancients, nor even from that middle age which abounded with many faults. Therefore although they may clatter, they will accomplish nothing by denying that they are insolent toward the Spirit of God as long as they transfer his power to fetid oil.

CR 35:502.

179. Martin Chemnitz (1522–1586), *Examination of the Council of Trent, On Confirmation,* 26 (1566)

This pertains to the second canon (*cf. #177 above*): We have already shown in many ways what kind of and how great a power they attribute to their chrism without any command and divine promise, and how great is the wrong and abuse of baptism to draw away that power from baptism and transfer it to the chrism, which has no word of God at all.

Preuss:297f.

180. Tilemann Hesshusen (1527–1588), *On the Errors of the Popes* 22,26

Chrism should not be so adored, if indeed the popes order that these words be said in the pontifical, "Hail, holy chrism." . . . .

Response: The whole doctrine of the popes concerning confirmation is a complete creation of the human brain without any testimony of sacred Scripture. . . . Idolatry and incantation, which is practiced in the magic consecration of chrism, is condemned in the first and second commandments. "You shall not have foreign gods before me. And you shall not take the name of the Lord your God in vain."

Sexcenti errores pleni blasphemiis in Deum quos Romana Pontificia Ecclesia contra Dei verbum furenter defendit. Frankfurt am Mainz: Georgius Coruinus, 1572. Fol. 111.

4

THE RECONCILIATION OF HERETICS

Even before confirmation split from baptism, the Church was developing a ritual expressed with similar imagery for the reconciliation of heretics.

Some had professed or been baptized in heresies distinct from the orthodox faith. If they chose to join the Church, they generally did so by a ritual anointing. Schismatics were generally reconciled by the imposition of a hand.

These gestures, perhaps omitted from heretical baptism, completed the ritual process and acted as symbols of conversion and membership to the new assembly of believers.

181. Origen (c. 185–253), *Homily on Leviticus* 8. 9

"Facing the Lord the priest sprinkles seven times with oil." For after these things which have been celebrated for the sake of purification, after he has repented and been reconciled to God, after the offerings of the ritual had been killed, he invites the sevenfold strength of the Holy Spirit upon him, according to him who said, "Give me the joy of your salvation, and confirm me with a dominant spirit."

Or certainly since the Lord witnesses in the Gospel that the hearts of sinners are besieged by "seven demons," "the priest facing the Lord" rightly "sprinkles seven times" in purification, that the expulsion of seven evil spirits from the purified heart may be declared, as "the oil is sprinkled out seven times by hand."

Therefore, through all these things we have spoken of above, purification is indeed thus given to those who have turned away from sin. But the gift of grace of the spirit is designated through the image of "oil," that the one who turns away from sin may not only find purification, but also be filled with the Holy Spirit. By the Holy Spirit he is both able to receive first the "stole and the ring," and, reconciled to the Father through everything, to be restored to the place of the son, through our very Lord Jesus Christ, to whom is glory and kingship for ever. Amen.

GCS 29:417.

182. Cyprian of Carthage (200?–258), *Letter* 70,2 (254–257?)

But the very questioning which happens in baptism is also a witness of the truth. For when we say, "Do you believe in eternal life and the forgiveness of sins through the holy Church?" we understand that the forgiveness of sins is not given except in the Church. But with heretics, where there is no Church sins are not forgiven. Therefore those who join heretics may either change the questioning or claim the truth, unless they ascribe "Church" to those whom they urge to have baptism.

It is also necessary that those who have been baptized be anointed, so that after the chrism (that is, the anointing) has been received, they have been anointed of God and have the grace of Christ in themselves. Afterwards at the eucharist oil has been sanctified on the altar, from which the baptized are anointed.

However, those who have neither the altar nor the Church cannot sanctify the creature of oil. For this reason, neither can there be a spiritual anointing among the heretics. When they state that the oil is sanctified and the eucharist is celebrated by them, it cannot be at all. But we ought to know and rememeber what has been written, "Let the oil of the sinner not anoint my head (Ps 141:5)."

CSEL 3,2:768.

183. Cyprian, *Letter* 72,1 (254–257?)

Some were baptized outside the Church and were spotted with the stain of profane water with the heretics and schismatics. When they come to us and to the Church which is one, it is necessary that they be baptized. It is equally fit to impose the hand on them for receiving the Holy Spirit, unless they also receive the baptism of the Church. For then they are finally able to be sanctified and to be children of God, if they are born by both sacraments, as has been written, "Unless one has been born of water and the spirit one cannot enter the reign of God."

CSEL 3,2:775.

184. *Cyprian (200–258), Letter to Jubajanus 1, 9 (256)*

(Cyprian defends his position favoring rebaptism. Some object that Acts does not support it, but he says the passage concerns another matter.)

Some people say concerning those who had been baptized in Samaria that when the apostles Peter and John arrived, the hand alone was imposed on them that they might receive the Holy Spirit; but they were not rebaptized at this place.

Most dear brother, we see that this instance does not pertain to the present cause at all. For those who had believed in Samaria believed with true faith, and had been baptized by Philip the deacon, whom the same apostles had sent, within the Church which is one, and to which alone it has been permitted to give the grace of baptism and to forgive sins. And therefore because they had followed the legitimate and ecclesiastical baptism, what they needed was not that they be baptized further, but only what was missing, which was done by Peter and John: By a prayer uttered for them and by the imposed hand, the Holy Spirit was invoked and was poured forth upon them.

Now this is also done among us, that those who are baptized in the Church are offered to the overseers of the Church, and through our prayer and the imposition of the hand they attain the Holy Spirit and are perfected by the sign of the Lord.

PL 3:1160.

185. Council of Arles I, canon 9 (or 8) (314)

Concerning Africans who use their own law to rebaptize, it is agreed that if people come to the Church from a heresy, the African faithful may ask them for the creed. If the faithful discern that the inquirers were baptized into the Father, the Son, and the Holy Spirit, only let the hand be imposed on them that they may receive the Holy Spirit. But if when asked for the creed they do not know this Trinity, let them be baptized.

CChr.SL 148:10-11.

186. Council of Nicaea, canon 31 (Arabic) (325)

If people convert to the orthodox faith, they must be received into the Church through the hands of a bishop, or of a presbyter, who ought to instruct them, that he might renounce all who act against the orthodox faith, and who speak against the apostolic Church. . . .

And after they have done these things, let the bishop receive them, or the priest to whose authority they pertain. Let him anoint them with the oil of chrism, and sign three times while anointing and while praying over them the prayer of Dionysius the Areopagite. Let prayer to God be made for them devoutly, that he may accept them.

And afterwards there will be the sharing of the divine sacraments of communion by which forgiveness of sins happens. If the one for whom these things have been done was a bishop, after his conversion he will remain at the degree of presbyter. If a presbyter, in the degree of deacon. If a deacon, in the degree of subdeacon. The same applies for the rest: They descend to the lower degree.

Mansi 2:962.

187. Council of Laodicea, canon 7 (c. 343–381)

Concerning those who return from heresies—Novatians, Photinians, or Quartodecimans—whether catechumens or faithful in these sects, let them not be received before having renounced all heresies, and in particular those they have left. Those among them who are called faithful in these sects may participate in the holy mystery, after having learned the creed of the faith and having been anointed with holy chrism.

Hefele 1:2, 999.

188. Augustine (354–430), *On Baptism* 5:1,1; 5:23,33 (400)

We use blessed Cyprian as a witness that the ancient custom of the catholic Church be now held, when people come from heretics or schismatics, if they have received a baptism consecrated with the evangelical words, they are not baptized again.

But if the imposition of the hand was not administered to people coming from a heresy, they are judged to be as those outside any fault. But because of the union of charity, which is the greatest gift of the Holy Spirit, without which the other holy things which are in a person have no strength for salvation, the hand is imposed on reformed heretics.

CSEL 51:261.290.

189. Theodoret (c. 393–466), *Compendium of Heretical Stories* 3,5 (453?)

The Novatians turn away from the sacred mysteries those who have entered second marriages, and they utterly banish the mention of penance from their assemblies. They do not offer the most holy chrism to those whom they baptize.

For these reasons the most praiseworthy Fathers ordered that those who are joined to the body of the Church from this heresy be anointed. Cornelius wrote many letters against this heresy, Dionysius the bishop of Alexander also wrote many, and also other bishops of that time. Through them the inhumanity of Novatus was at once made manifest to all.

PG 83:407f.

190. Theodoret, *Interpretation of the Letter to the Hebrews* 6:4-6 (453–466?)

"For it is impossible that those who were once enlightened, who had tasted the heavenly gift, and were made sharers of the Holy Spirit, who had tasted the good word of God and the powers of the coming age—and who had lapsed, to be restored again for penance, and to make a show of crucifying themselves again to the Son of God."

It is not able to happen at all, he says, that those who approached most holy baptism, and were sharers of the grace of the divine Spirit, and received a foreshadowing of eternal goods, may approach again and pursue another baptism. For this is nothing other than to crucify the Son of God again, and to bring about with disgrace the same things which had earlier been brought about.

PG 82:715-718.

191. Pope Leo I (440–461), *Letter* 159, 7

Those who received baptism from heretics since they had not been baptized before, should be confirmed by the sole invocation of the Holy Spirit through the imposition of hands, because they have received only the form of baptism without the strength of sanctification.

PL 54:1138f.

192. Pope Leo I, *Letter* 166, 2

If it has been established that people were baptized by heretics, in no way will the sacrament of regeneration be repeated for them. But only that may be conferred which was absent there—that they may pursue the strength of the Holy Spirit through the episcopal imposition of the hand.

PL 54:1194.

193. Council of Arles II, canon 17 (442–506)

It is clear that the followers of Bonoso, coming from the same error, baptize into the Trinity like the Arians. If when asked they confess our faith with their whole heart, it suffices that they be received in the Church with chrism and the imposition of hands.

CChr.SL 148:117.

194. Gennadius (+ c. 492), *Book of Ecclesiastical Dogmas* 21

"There is one baptism," but in the Church where "there is one faith," where it is given "in the name of the Father and of the Son and of the Holy Spirit." And therefore if those who were baptized by those heretics who baptize in the confession of the holy Trinity come also to us, they are indeed received as baptized, lest the invocation of the holy Trinity or the confession be annulled. But they are taught first and instructed in what sense the mystery of the holy Trinity is held in the Church. If they agree to believe or assent to confess, purged now by the integrity of faith, they may be confirmed with the imposition of the hand.

But if they are children or dullards who do not understand doctrine, those may respond for them who offer them according to the custom of those needing to be baptized. Thus they may be admitted to the mysteries of the eucharist by the imposition of the hand and the chrism of the strong.

But those who were baptized by heretics not in the invocation of the holy Trinity and come to us—we pronounce that they ought to be baptized. Not rebaptized, for it must not be believed that they had been baptized who were not immersed in the name of the Father and the Son and the holy Spirit according to the rule imposed by the Lord: as are the following: the Paulianites, the Proclians, the Borborites, the Sipurs, the Fotiniacs (who now are called Bonosians), the Montanists, and the Manicheans—the shoots of impiety having been diversified. Or as are the rest of them, plagues of origin or order which introduce two elements unknown to themselves, like Cerdo and Marcion. Or elements opposed, like Manicheus. Or three elements, like Theudotus. Or many, like Valentinus. Or that Christ was a man but not God, like Cerinthus, Ebion, Artemon, and Fotinus. I say if any come to us from these, it need not be sought from them whether or not they were baptized, but this only, if they believe the faith of the Church, and let them be baptized by ecclesiastical baptism.

JThS 7,25:93f.

195. Pope Vigilius I (537–555), *Letter* 1, 3 (538?)

The reconciliation of Arians is done not through that imposition of the hand which happens through the invocation of the Holy Spirit, but through that by which the fruit of penitence is acquired and perfected with the restitution of holy communion.

PL 69:18.

196. Pope Gregory I (590–604), *Epistle* 67, *Book* 11

We have taught from the ancient institution of the Fathers that those who are baptized in a heresy in the name of the Trinity, if they return to the holy Church, may be recalled to the womb of mother Church either by the anointing of chrism, or by the imposition of hands, or by a mere profession of faith. For this reason, the West restores Arians to the door of the catholic Church through the imposition of hands, but the East through the anointing of sacred chrism.

But the Church receives Monophysites and others by a simple profession because it accepts in them the holy baptism of cleansing, which they once pursued with the heretics. So either the former will have received the Holy Spirit through the imposition of the hand, or the latter will have been united to the heart of the holy and universal Church through the profession of the true faith.

CIC 1:1380. (Gratian, c. 44, D. 4, de cons.)

197. Gratian (12th c.), *Second part of the Decretal, Cause 1, Canon 58, Question 1*

Behold, when baptism is received with its strength from heretics, its administration is so necessary, that once given it may not even be repeated by pagans. For this reason it is read in the Ecclesiastical History that Alexander the Bishop of Alexandria, when he celebrated the solemnities of Peter the Martyr, after the sacraments of the Mass were finished, saw upon the shore of the sea the play of children, imitating the bishop, as they were accustomed, and wearing those things which are usually worn in church.

He immediately ordered them to be brought to him, and he questioned them strictly what they had done. They related the situation; they confessed that certain catechumens had been baptized by them through the boy Athanasius, who had pretended to be the bishop for them.

When he saw from their answers that all things fit the rite of our religion, he told those on whom water had been poured since their questions and answers were sound, that they should not be baptized again, but those rites which are customary for priests should be finished.

CIC 1:380.

198. Martin Chemnitz (1522–1586), *Examination of the Council of Trent, On Confirmation, 24,6 (1566)*

Augustine clearly is speaking about returning heretics and schismatics. But Augustine answers how charity may be inspired by the imposition of the hand: "The imposition of the hand is nothing else but a prayer over a person. Therefore, unlike baptism, it cannot be repeated" (*cf. #50 above*). And Gratian says concerning that sentence of Augustine in 1 quaest. 1 cap. Arianos: "He shows it is not a sacrament when he orders that the imposition of hands is repeated." Therefore whatever passages are cited from ancient writers are different and diverse from pontifical confirmation, as it was described above.

Preuss:297.

Index